DESTINED TO FAIL

A MEMOIR OF RESILIENCE

ANAS AFANA
WITH STELLA BELLOW

LANDON
HAIL
PRESS

Copyright © 2022 Anas Afana
All Rights Reserved

Paperback ISBN 979-8-9863282-3-2
Hardback ISBN: 979-8-9863282-4-9

Published by Landon Hail Press

Disclaimer: This work depicts actual events in the life of the author as truthfully as recollection permits and/or can be verified by research. Occasionally, dialogue consistent with the character, nature of the person speaking, or their native language has been supplemented and/or translated. All persons within are actual individuals; there are no composite characters. The names of some individuals have been changed to respect their privacy.

For my children, Nader and Danah

DESTINED TO FAIL

CONTENTS

PART ONE The Past Life: 1984-1993	3
RIOT	5
IMMUNITY	24
THE BRIBE	35
PUBLIC SCHOOL	50
HITCHHIKERS	64
YOU HAVE WHAT IT TAKES	94
THE CORNFIELDS	108
PART TWO Survival Mode: 1993-2014	123
THE NIGHTMARE	125
LIFELINES	134
ILLEGAL SURVIVAL	149
REUNION	173
THE ACCOMPLISHMENT	188
FEVER DREAM	199
A YEAR AND A HALF	224
BLUR	245

MI FAMILIA ESPAÑOLA	256
EIGHTEEN YEARS LATER	273
ROCK BOTTOM	293
PART THREE Becoming the Pirate: 2014-2019	303
STAN DARLING	305
THE PIRATE	323
THE LAUNCH	338
GOOD INTENTIONS	358
PASS THE BATON	365
ACKNOWLEDGMENTS	371
ABOUT THE AUTHORS	374

PART ONE
THE PAST LIFE: 1984-1993

ANAS AFANA & STELLA BELLOW

DESTINED TO FAIL

RIOT

I never told my friends about my childhood. Even into my mid-forties, I held onto my secrets, which hid themselves in the caverns of my subconscious. I seldom let anyone in.

Despite my being guarded, people were crucial fixtures in my life. I loved my friends, especially the close ones. I didn't keep my past from them because I thought they weren't worthy of knowing. Rather, when I was seventeen, I had to forge a new self. I was left in the middle of the United States, amidst the dense quiet cornfields, with some cash, a summer jacket, and not much else. Between my gravely underpaid jobs and the shock of a new existence, I was deeply frightened.

I grew up a child of privilege. My family moved around a lot. My dad was big and important. He made certain we were provided for, and we were comfortable. I saw sublime regions of the world, met powerful people, and went on adventures with my friends. I loved soccer, and during my teenage years, I was recruited to a professional team in Jordan. But I never had a chance to play. Instead, I found myself a teenager in a foreign country, fumbling with a language I didn't speak and fighting to survive.

My childhood was the only time when I had true autonomy. Being my father's son growing up made me untouchable. But at seventeen, that version of myself was no more–I became cynical and scared. Once I was displaced to the United States, I shut out my childhood back in the Middle East. I lied about it, too. No one knew who my dad was or that I had ever been comfortable. Being deserted in the Midwest left me vulnerable, an exposed thing in the wilderness. I had to save myself.

Now, I am forty-six, and my brain whirs in my sleep. I am content with the life I have built. For a Jordanian-American dental technician who lives in Nebraska, however, it has become overwhelming to reconcile it all. I saw my existence in two parts. The latter is great and terrifying and ever-unfolding.

The first, I love and know by heart....

At ten years old, I watched the outside hurtle past as the plane roared down the tarmac. My mom grew pale, gripping the armrest as we went perpendicular. Jordan became a faint, golden speck below us. We were bound for Sudan, where my dad, the diplomat, awaited us.

I was nine years younger than my three siblings–my oldest sister was twenty-two; my brother and sisters were away at university. More or less, I grew up an only child.

DESTINED TO FAIL

My parents and I had only been home in Amman for a year when my dad announced his promotion. Before that, we had lived on the thirty-sixth floor of an apartment complex in Paris, where my dad was the charge d'affaires of Jordan from 1983 to 1985.

Europe in the eighties was rife with the mysterious assassinations of Jordanian diplomats. Paris was a high-profile, reputable city with a large concentration of embassies. In the eighties, it became a geopolitical hunting ground, where several of these assassinations of Middle Eastern and Jordanian diplomats took place. The numbers of fatalities rose, but no one knew by how many exactly. My mom and I weren't allowed to open the door for anyone, only for a security guard or if someone we knew knocked with a secret rhythm. I grew up with high security.

Reports of dead ambassadors and hijacked airplanes glued my father to the television. Open secrets circulated around the Middle East. The notorious deep-state intelligence agency from one contested country sent spies to lurk in every corner of the world, and mercenaries were paid by certain governments to participate in covert attacks. My dad had theories, but no person or entity was ever held to account. A dead diplomat was merely a pawn in some statement or retaliation. My dad, fearing he and his family were next, was constantly paranoid and always carried at least one loaded handgun.

In the weeks after my father announced to us his promotion to be ambassador of Jordan and his reassignment to Khartoum, my mom and I watched the news. Volatility was everywhere: riots and starving children, under a corrupt, oppressive government. My mom stewed in despair, a contagion that latched onto me, as time seemed to stand still in the sky.

I was used to the temporary: I'd gone to a different school every few years, made new friends, and then bid them goodbye. I had Jordanian friends and French friends, and now I'd have Sudanese friends. I hoped they played football and tried to reassure myself about the whole thing. *Sudan can't be as bad as they say it is*, I thought.

As I looked out the window, hues of warm earth and sand were vivid beneath us, disrupted by two arms, emerald and snakelike, the tributaries of the Nile.

My heart raced as we descended on the desert. When the plane landed, my mom and I stood up with the other passengers. The doors opened, and everyone gasped for air. I felt a monstrous wave of heat wash over me like water.

My dad squinted up at my mom and me from the bottom of the airstair. He had a powerful head of black hair with a streak of white that ran along his part and barely lifted in the stagnant air. The faint skyline behind him seemed washed out by yellow dust.

DESTINED TO FAIL

When she saw my dad, my mom made noises of horror, her eyes darting around. "Where have you brought me?" she cried out. "To *hell?*"

As we drove together to our new house, I was wide-eyed, trying to take it all in. The desert was a sepia blanket that covered all the houses and roads. The buildings were golden-brown, and the signs and storefronts were orange, green, and piercing teal. Heaps of trash littered the roadside. Small, rickety buses clambered past us, their insides packed and the tops crowded with young men who'd climbed a ladder up the side. I pressed my nose to the window in awe.

The car pulled up to the gates of our new house. We would discover that one of the benefits of being an ambassador was having a house kept up by servants, though royal treatment was not something my mom and I were used to. A guard sat in a booth by the gates of the house and stood up in reverence of my dad, when we pulled up in our car. The driver honked at a servant to open the gates.

The house was a large, one-story villa with a flat roof and a spacious front yard. As the three of us came through the front door, my dad flicked the switch, but no lights came on. It was hotter inside than out.

My mom looked at him. "What's going on?"

"There's no power. It only comes on for about six hours a day."

"What do you mean?" she asked. "I can't live like this. It's too hot."

"We'll have to start the generator," said my dad, referring to the giant hunk of metal in our yard. A network of copper tubes and radiators, it was our sole source of power. One of the servants dashed outside and cranked the machine until it emitted black smoke and made sounds like a firearm. Suddenly, the lights in the front room turned on. Still, the noise drowned out the hum of the air-conditioner.

"What is *this*?" my mom asked. "Is it always going to be this loud?"

"Yeah," said my dad. "If you want power."

The house was either baking because of the flat roof that the sun beat down on or noisy because of the generator. We learned that it would stay on for about six hours max and turn off at random. Often, every machine in the neighborhood would be firing all at once, creating a collective roar.

Our disquiet lingered into the next day. My dad adapted the same paranoia he'd had in Paris. Although Khartoum would prove to be much safer for a Jordanian diplomat and his family, we were in a new, unstable country, and he imposed strict safety measures. I couldn't go anywhere on my own, and my parents had to know where I was at all times. As the child of a prominent figure, I was always the potential object of a kidnapping.

DESTINED TO FAIL

Once my parents' nerves settled, my dad showed me the neighborhood, while my mom stayed home to unpack. The chauffeur drove us down a street riddled with potholes and lined with embassies and consulates. The flag of one waved at the flag of another from across the way, while members of the Sudanese military acted as watchmen out front. The driver turned out of our neighborhood onto Madani Street, the busy, four-lane road that connected all of Khartoum. The median was a sandy ditch, and the buildings alongside it were flat, huddled under the immense sky.

As we drove along, the number of storefronts dwindled before disappearing completely. We continued on until a building rolled into view on our left. The sunlight glinted off the iron gates of the American Embassy. The embassies in my neighborhood were modest and squat. By contrast, this was a palace, a compound that occupied half the street, the equivalent of an entire city block.

We passed the embassy and turned right. A few kilometers farther, a foreboding brick fortress towered above us, its windows shattered and toothy, surrounded by a concrete wall. The entrance was a metal gate with bars that formed spikes.

"This is your school," said my dad.

I almost crapped myself. "Are you sure this is the right place?"

"I'm sure," he said flatly. "It's an Egyptian private school. Public schools are not an option. This is one of the better ones I could find."

One of the better ones? I thought. I already felt the oppressive brick walls close in. It took all I had to say to him, "Dad, I don't want to go here."

"Deal with it."

I wasn't permitted to argue.

I started school a week later. My mom packed a sandwich and a bottle of water next to my books and insisted I drink nothing from the school. She waved goodbye as the chauffeur pulled onto the road. The morning light illuminated the route, which had grown more familiar. We passed the American Embassy, turned the corner, and arrived at school five minutes later.

Crowds of Sudanese and Egyptian students made their way through the metal gates, speaking to one another in the local dialect of Arabic my mom and I were still learning. I swung my backpack over my shoulder and said goodbye to the driver. My breath quickened as I walked into the jaws of the Egyptian private school.

The first teacher walked into class with a cigarette hanging from his mouth. The teacher who taught the next class lit the end of one, too, but the smell was not of tobacco. It was nauseating, like burning rubber. Every teacher there smoked, something Jordanian teachers wouldn't dream of doing. They had clean rooms, sustainable salaries, and

DESTINED TO FAIL

unviolated windows. In Sudan, the teachers' smoking seemed justified.

In the first few weeks of school, I made a few friends. All the students there were North African; the majority were Sudanese, and the minority were Egyptian. I was the only non-North African in school, and especially in the beginning, I was intimidated. It was during that time that I met Mustafa. He was a year older than I, long-faced and lanky. Mustafa was the son of the Iraqi ambassador, and he knew the life of armored vehicles and bodyguards. My dad had given me instructions to look for the other ambassador's son. When he walked into class, I waved him over. Mustafa liked football as much as I did, and we became fast friends.

In the morning, two days after Mustafa's arrival, faint chanting rang from the street. As the sounds of a crowd grew closer, my classmates slipped their books into their backpacks and prepared to leave. Then, outside, they grew raucous in excitement and called, "*Riot!*"

Mustafa and I were the baffled newcomers. We locked eyes. "Riot?"

I looked out the window, where a crowd rallied around the school walls. They were mostly students, ranging from preteens to twenty-somethings. Some held signs, while others wielded sharp rocks. They swung their arms in preparation of pelting the windows with the stones, insisting the gates be opened so the students could leave school to join them. At that point, I barely understood the Sudanese dialect. On a few signs, however, I recognized the word, *Libya*.

The gates never opened. We heard a sound like heavy rain against the school and then breaking glass. Rocks flew in through the open windows and hit the walls and desks. Mustafa and I crouched, covering our heads. I realized why so many windows were broken. This kind of stuff happened here all the time.

The teacher knew the drill. "You two, go to the bathroom in the courtyard," he said. "Keep quiet until the riot passes."

The other kids had been anxious to get out and join the protest. Now, they were angry—at the rocks, at the teacher, and at the round object that sailed through the window a moment later that began to hiss and shake, threatening to combust.

"*Bomban!*" one of the students yelled.

"What did he say?" Mustafa asked me.

"Tear gas bomb!" the teacher shouted.

Before we could react, the bomb exploded. My eardrums rang as the room filled with a yellow fog. The kids closest to it screamed and coughed, and Mustafa and I stumbled about. The room grew invisible. Some kids crowded around the door, while the desperate ones jumped from the second-floor classroom onto the ground below, heedless of injury.

DESTINED TO FAIL

"We've gotta get out of here," Mustafa said with a cough.

Tears streamed down to our chins as we felt around for the door. The sting in my eyes was unbearable. I thought I'd go blind.

"Follow me to the bathroom!" I cried.

We squeezed through the crowd so one of us could prise the door open. Then we flew down the hall, gasping for fresh air. My eyes stung and my vision of the schoolyard was blurry.

Mustafa and I locked ourselves in the outdoor bathroom and rushed to the sinks, where we washed our faces, flushed our eyes, and rinsed water around our mouths for twenty minutes. Eventually, our tears subsided. The bathroom was rank, but I would have taken the scent of feces over tear gas any day. Mustafa and I cracked the door open and stuck out our noses, taking desperate whiffs of the untainted air outside.

For a while, we sat there, listening to the riot grow distant until the school was silent. Perhaps forty-five minutes passed before we looked at each other and realized we were the only ones there. *The gates must have been opened,* I thought. We walked out of the bathroom and stood there in the hall for a moment.

"You think we should call someone?" Mustafa asked.

"Where would we find a phone?" I said.

"Principal's office maybe?"

I scrunched my nose. "I bet it's locked. We could check, though."

Mustafa and I strolled through the empty building, poking our heads into classrooms in search of a phone, but to no avail. Through the windows, we saw the riot move toward Madani Street. Our last resort was the principal's office. We took turns shaking the handle, but the door wouldn't budge.

"Crap," I said.

I knew Khartoum a little. At least, I knew the route to school. But Mustafa was fresh. He had been in Sudan for a mere forty-eight hours.

"We should go to the American Embassy," I said, assuredly. The idea of venturing outside worried me, but there would be powerful adults there to take care of us. We could call our parents from there, and we would be safe.

"I think I know where that is," Mustafa replied. "But isn't it far? If we go outside, we could get seriously hurt. We should probably wait for someone to come help us."

"No one's coming. Not now," I said. "And we can't wait here for five hours for the driver to pick us up. What happens if the rioters come back? What if they throw more bombs at us? What if someone lights the school on fire? We can't stay here. We'll be safe at the Embassy."

Mustafa didn't like the idea of leaving. He also didn't want to be left alone. "Where do you think the rioters are going?"

"I don't know," I said. "They're probably going to the palace or to some government building. I really think we should try to reach the American Embassy, because it's in the other direction. We'll take the back way to avoid the crowd."

For a moment, Mustafa struggled with the thought. "What about our bags?"

"Leave them," I said. "We need to run."

He sighed. "Okay."

We walked out the front door and ran toward an alley. The dark path led to the uneven side streets that surrounded the intersection between the school and the American Embassy. Alleys were separated by houses, backyards, and flatlands of sand, all divided by tall fences.

Our path was somewhat diagonal. The next thirty minutes was an obstacle course. We jumped over fences, scurried across someone's property, sprinted over a hot desert flatland, then dove into another alleyway. At ten and eleven, we had endless stamina.

Once, a man caught sight of Mustafa as he ran through his backyard and called out to him. "Hey! Get out of my yard!"

Mustafa was startled. I saw his eyes widen as the man approached him with a large stick. Mustafa fled, leaping over the fence I had just scaled. The man hurled curses as we ran. "Damn white kids!"

We went unnoticed as we scurried through the next yard. At ten in the morning, it felt like one hundred degrees. We were drenched in sweat.

"We should've brought our water," Mustafa said, winded.

He and I crossed a two-way street that was almost empty of cars, then jumped another fence and ran down another alley. I could see black smoke billowing over the rooftops ahead and steered west to avoid it. We stopped to catch our breath behind a wall.

I knew we had reached Madani Street. The chanting was there again, this time mingled with the smell of burning tires. *What are they doing here?* I wondered. I peered from the alley and could see the riot raging in front of the embassy. Stuff like wood and tires had caught fire, while tear gas bombs went off, and rubble littered the street. The crowd seemed endless; it stretched from the northeast wall of the embassy down Madani Street, past the right turn to our school.

Because I had diverted us, I'd overshot the route. We were past the U.S. Embassy, and to reach, it we'd have to cross at an angle. Mustafa and I were thirsty and overheated; we needed water and air-conditioning. We realized we couldn't turn back now, and we had to cross the highway.

A Sudanese guard sat in a protected booth attached to the gates of the embassy, where he was monitoring the

DESTINED TO FAIL

rioters. In hopes he would notice us, Mustafa and I crept a little ways out from our hiding place, then jumped up and down, furiously waving our arms. After a few minutes, the guard spotted us. He knew we were in trouble.

He put up his arms. *Stay where you are,* he signaled.

The guard said something into his handheld radio. He lifted and cocked his machine gun then left his booth, aiming the weapon at the rioters. The threat sent the crowd down the street in a wave of shouts. Once they were far enough away, his automatic still pointed in their direction, the guard gave us a meaningful stare. With his head, he beckoned. *Come over.*

Mustafa and I ran at a right angle toward the embassy. The automatic held the protesters a few extra meters away. The gates screeched open, just enough for a ten- and eleven-year-old to worm their way through. As we ran, the rioters saw they had been fooled. They shouted to one another and pelted us and the guard with rocks.

I heard Mustafa beside me as I kept my eyes on the guard, who retreated back into his booth. He still gestured to us. *Run!*

We reached the first and second highway lanes. As we neared the stretch of sand in the middle of the road, sharp rocks whizzed past and pummeled the ground a few feet from our upturned heels. We scrambled across the ditch in the middle of the road without thinking about the sand in our shoes. Then we picked up speed. Mustafa and I crossed the third and fourth lanes. As the embassy grew nearer, so did the rioters. The rocks rained closer, too.

When we reached the gates, I dove onto American soil, with Mustafa quite literally on top of me. I was almost grateful for his elbow in my eye. The gates clanged shut, and we heard the rocks drum on the tall walls that surrounded the compound. I exhaled, my heart still pounding. Mustafa and I checked ourselves for injuries, but we weren't cut or bruised from the rocks. None had hit us as we ran.

The embassy itself sat in the distance, a testament to how enormous the compound was. We breathed: *we're safe*. Several guards, including the one who helped Mustafa and me, gathered around in confusion.

"What were you *doing*?" the guard scolded.

"We ran from our school," I said. I explained how the protesters rallied at our school and we had escaped when the building emptied. I told the guard about my father, that we were ten and eleven, children of ambassadors and new to the school and the country. We had found ourselves in a bad situation.

"We decided to come here, where it was safe."

"You two did the right thing." The guard nodded. "You're safe now. We'll call your fathers and drive you home once things quiet down."

DESTINED TO FAIL

Mustafa and I thanked him. He spoke into his radio and walked back to his post. The other guards walked with us to the embassy, and we were ushered inside.

Save for the Sudanese guards and one or two others, the inside of the U.S. Embassy was unusually empty. Where my dad worked at the Jordanian Embassy, phones rang, people rushed to and fro, and offices clamored with typewriters in use.

"Where *is* everybody?" I asked. A guard told me all the important people had been flown out due to a violent incident. I didn't ask anything else.

Mustafa and I stayed on the upper floors, safe inside the American palace. Destruction erupted outside as we sipped juice. We heard screams from the street below and saw black smoke. By midday, the riots were over.

"That didn't happen like I thought it would," I said. "Why were the rioters here, anyway?"

"I don't know," said Mustafa. "Told you we should've stayed at school. But this embassy is really nice, and running here was fun. Before the rocks."

Soon, two guards appeared and escorted us through the gates. Traffic had slowly resumed on Madani Street. An American and a Sudanese guard stood by an armored Jeep.

"Is this car safe?" I asked. The question was insincere; I was just being clever. One of the guards smiled and rolled down a window. The width of the glass was four fingers thick.

A Sudanese driver took us home, while the American guard sat on the passenger's side, a gun in his holster. When we pulled up to the house, my parents were waiting by the gate. I got out of the Jeep.

My mom squeezed me. "Thank God you're safe. I was so scared." She turned to my father. "We're going home," she said, vehemently. "First thing tomorrow!"

He ignored her and engaged in somber conversation with the American guard. Mustafa emerged from the Jeep, and the guard left. Mustafa's father, another hardened diplomat, arrived a few minutes later. While my mom made tea, Mustafa and I recounted the adventure, interrupting each other in excitement. We told them about our mad dash through backyards and how the old man threatened Mustafa with a stick. Mustafa and I laughed from our bellies as we recalled his futile rage. Our dads, men of stone, didn't think it was funny.

We reached the part about walking into the American Embassy, and I told them how empty it was.

"That's most likely to do with the situation between America and Libya," said my dad.

"What happened?" asked Mustafa.

"The Americans bombed Benghazi," said his father. "Then, an employee at the embassy here was shot. All the diplomats were recalled to America."

"That may have had something to do with the location of the protest," said my dad.

DESTINED TO FAIL

To seek refuge at the American Embassy was good thinking. But I was ten and, of course, could never have known about the situation with Libya. Before the two of them left, Mustafa's father looked down at me.

"Thank you for taking Mustafa to the embassy," he said. "After this, you two will be the best of friends."

My mom was still shaken up when I went to bed. She asked if I had been scared. Running through side streets and backyards had been thrilling. We had seen enough movies to fancy ourselves daring adventurers. It was only when we'd gotten to the highway that we'd been really frightened. I'd barely registered the size of the rocks but knew one to the scalp would have rendered me unconscious. At ten, I suddenly knew what danger was. I had felt it whizz past my nose and land by my feet.

"What are we doing here?" I asked my mom.

"I don't know," she said, wearily. "This is our life."

I figured the rioters must have thought we were Americans. If they'd known we were Iraqi and Jordanian, they wouldn't have pelted us with rocks.

We learned how to be inconspicuous from the Sudanese kids, who were no strangers to the riots. Word circulated in the days before the next eruptions. My new friends would let me know in shouted whispers, *"Psst,* hey! Riot this Thursday!"

I would tell my parents, and they trusted the intel. On those days, they let me stay home.

IMMUNITY

During school, Mustafa told me his dad had let him learn how to drive. Their chauffeur had taught him. I was jealous. I didn't know much about our family driver—just that his name was Ali, and he had a small apartment on the embassy property, where he lived on weekdays. When my parents needed him, they called him through an intercom.

I figured we were pals at that point, so I piped up to him one day. "I want you to teach me how to drive."

Ali laughed nervously. "You're kidding, right?"

"Mustafa knows how to drive. Why can't you teach me?"

"Because," he said, like he thought it was obvious, "I don't want to lose my job."

"You won't," I said. "We'll keep it a secret."

"If I don't teach you, there'll be no secrets to keep," Ali said. He meant to end the conversation.

"What about money?" I suggested. "I can pay you. No one has to know."

DESTINED TO FAIL

"How much?" Ali chuckled. "You're only ten. You probably don't have much to give me."

I didn't like when grown-ups were condescending. "I'll use my allowance. How does five pounds per lesson sound?"

He paused, and I held my breath.

"Fine," he sighed. "But I'm going to need more than what you're offering."

I hid my glee. "Sure. Name a fair price."

"Twenty pounds per lesson," Ali said. "I'll teach you everything."

"Twenty is too much," I said. I had learned to haggle from my mom, who was master of it.

"Then how about ten pounds?" Ali asked.

"Either five pounds or I'll go to Mustafa's driver and pay him instead."

Ali caved. "All right. It's a deal."

I extended my hand from the backseat, and Ali shook it.

After school the next day, Ali drove me to a sandy flatland a little ways from the airport. The desert stretched on for miles. It was spacious and silent, save for the occasional swoosh of an airplane engine in the distance. Slow heat rose from the sand. The sky turned orange as the sun descended.

Ali had brought a square, stiff cushion that set me a few inches above the dashboard. He took out the keys but first withheld them. "Careful," he said. "Follow my instructions."

I nodded as I took the keys and turned them in the ignition. The engine sputtered to life.

After a month of lessons, I had improved. When I'd gained enough experience shifting gears, Ali stopped teaching me. He took naps in the passenger's seat while I drove in circles for half an hour in the afternoons. I cackled as the car flew through the desert, kicking up yellow dust in our wake.

One day, Ali's head drooped predictably onto his chest. When my joy ride was over, I looked over at him. He was still asleep, his breathing deep and peaceful. *What if I just drove home?* I thought. I would have to drive off the flatland and onto the highway. It was against the rules, but I didn't care.

I meandered out of the flatland, peering over at Ali in case he woke up. For a few death-defying moments, I crossed the highway then took the way home through the quiet neighborhoods. Halfway through the drive, I thought of my dad. Perhaps he was on his way out of work or sat at home, expectant. *I should pull over.*

I parked on the side of the street and gently shook Ali's shoulder. He slowly blinked himself to consciousness. When he saw the road, the other cars, and a ten-year-old in the driver's seat, he nearly jumped.

"Where am I?" he shouted. "What did you do?"

"I just drove us close to home," I said. "You can drive the last two blocks, so my dad doesn't see me."

"Never do that again!"

For three days, Ali revoked my driving privileges. I desperately wanted another joy-ride, so I promised not to disobey him again. Soon, Ali trusted me, and I proved to him I could handle the responsibility of a car.

A few weeks later, I received a summons from my dad. I walked into the living room with a familiar dread, thinking, *He knows about the driving.*

My dad handed me a laminated card.

"What's it for?" I asked. My own face stared up at me. Beside it read *Diplomat*. I turned it over and read this statement, in bold letters: *The carrier of this card cannot be arrested or prosecuted.*

I thought, *Whoa.*

"I looked into this after the riots," my dad said. "It's diplomatic immunity."

"Okay," I said.

"Don't lose it. Keep it on you all the time."

The next day at school, I secretly showed the card to Mustafa. He showed me the one he had.

I grinned. "We should have some fun."

My diplomatic ID

I gradually realized the power of diplomatic immunity: I couldn't get into any trouble with that card in my pocket. I thought of the gated clubs around Khartoum. They were exclusive and international, abundant in courtyards and swimming pools and upscale restaurants reserved for the wealthy.

All diplomats stationed in Sudan and their families were part of a country club. My family and Mustafa's belonged to the same one. We went there for parties and family gatherings and played football with the other children of diplomats.

DESTINED TO FAIL

Playing football in Sudan

On one occasion, my parents and I were invited to a club reserved for Sudanese Army soldiers, veterans, and their families. For non-members, it was by invitation only. My dad saw it as a dull formality, but my mom and I looked forward to it. At the military club, I ordered the fish. It was the best meal of my life. I inhaled lemony goodness, and savored every bite. As we were leaving, I saw the club my family frequented in the distance. I realized the two shared a fence.

For a week after the event, the fish drifted through my mind. I wanted it again. When I saw Mustafa at the country club, I relayed a devious plan to him.

Mustafa looked at me like I'd swallowed a goat. "You're crazy," he said.

"Would you relax," I said. "I've got enough money for both of us. If we get found out, we'll show our diplomat cards and leave. Live a little!"

We made sure no eyes were on us. Mustafa and I climbed the fence using a scraggly tree branch for support. We landed cautiously on our feet.

"We're gonna get caught," Mustafa said under his breath.

"No, we're not," I said, nervously. "Just don't look so scared."

We walked into the restaurant of the military club, where the majority were Sudanese people, some in uniform, talking and eating. We were two olive-skinned kids, so our appearance was a little odd. But people of different nationalities were invited there often, and nobody suspected us. We pretended to have a conversation as we sat down. The waiter walked over, and asked for our order.

"The fish," I said. "Two orders, please."

Mustafa and I fidgeted as we waited, trying to look inconspicuous. A stern man in uniform approached us.

He towered over our table. "Hello. Welcome," he said. "Who are you here with?"

I quickly scanned the restaurant. My eyes landed on a table of white people across the room.

"There they are!" I said. "Those are our parents."

DESTINED TO FAIL

The man in uniform politely nodded. "Enjoy your meal."

Soon, the steaming fish landed in front of us. As Mustafa and I ate, we ascended into a different dimension. We made noises of satisfaction and were sad when we reached the last bite.

"If I could eat the bones, I would," Mustafa drawled, blissfully.

I left the total amount plus a tip, and we casually walked out of the restaurant. We scaled the fence again and met our unsuspecting parents back at the country club.

I detested school, where I was constrained by desks and chairs. In my first year in Sudan, football ingrained itself in my muscle memory and occupied my mind. I played with my friends every weekend and kicked a ball around whenever there was time.

Often, it was too hot to play outside. Sudan was an organism that oozed heat. On street corners, passersby drank from clay pots of water with a tin cup that sat on the lid. My parents positioned two under a tree in our yard. At noon, the low-hanging sun was deadliest. The adults warned me not to play in the middle of the day, only mornings and evenings before sunset. The thick, suffocating heat we'd felt when the plane landed was constant. I never truly acclimated to it.

In the last days of the school year, my mom and I prepared to leave for Jordan. The arrangement was for her and me to see family in the summer and then fly back to Khartoum for the start of the new school year. My dad stayed behind at his post in Sudan, because the ambassadorial position required his constant availability.

I said goodbye to Mustafa and my new friends. I was sad to leave but excited to see everyone back home, especially Cousin Razi.

When my mom and I walked through the Khartoum airport, our bags weren't checked by security. We walked up the stairs onto the plane with our red passports and sat first class. At the edge of my seat was an ashtray. I thought of the Egyptian teachers at my private school, who taught with a piece of chalk in one hand and a smoldering cigarette in the other. They often complained about their cigarettes, as the ones they could afford to smoke were the Sudanese kind, cheap and second-rate. They dreamed of nice foreign cigarettes, brands that were nonexistent in Sudan. These were too expensive and out of reach of the working class.

Huh, I thought. *Jordanian cigarettes have gotta be better than the ones here. My teachers would love them. And I have a magical diplomat card that saves me from getting in trouble. I could make something from this.*

The cunning thoughts compounded. A bag perfect for smuggling Jordanian cigarettes. The knack for negotiation I inherited from my mom. My teachers, underpaid and addicted to nicotine. My poor grades, which could go up with some haggling.

I mulled it over as I sat next to my unsuspecting mother. We settled in, and the flight attendant glided through the aisle to greet us.

There were no direct flights from Khartoum to Amman; our connection was in Cairo, where we spent a day's layover. My mom and I toured the city and stayed the night at a hotel. The flight to Jordan took an hour and fifteen minutes. Finally, we arrived in our neighborhood in Amman, where we lived as normal citizens. There were no bodyguards and little cause for worry. My mom relaxed.

When Razi and I saw each other, we shouted for joy and hugged. I was the center of attention upon my return. "What's *Sudan* like?" my friends asked, their eyes wide. We all sat on the curb as I told them about the riots in elaborate detail.

"And then we *dove* through the gates into the American Embassy," I said. Their mouths hung open, and they asked if I was serious. When I told them I could drive, their eyes widened. Some were skeptical.

"Sure, and I can *fly*," one of them retorted. He took a drag of a cigarette, and nodded in my direction. "Prove it."

I seized my opportunity one day, when my mom was out of the house. I set a pillow on the driver's seat. For fifteen minutes, I took everyone for a spin around the neighborhood. My friends laughed and squealed as I turned corners. They groaned in disappointment when I said I had to drop them back off and park the car where I'd found it. I drove home, and my mom never knew.

Whenever I was in downtown Amman, I picked up a few packs of cigarettes. The age requirement was nonexistent. The cigarettes were unexceptional, a Jordanian brand. My allowance was three dinars, worth lots more in Sudan than in Jordan. For the next three months, I accumulated packs with my allowance. By the time summer was over, I had twenty packs of cigarettes. I stashed them in the boiler room, where nobody went. On our last night in Jordan, I placed the cigarettes in my suitcase, covered them with my clothes, and shut my bag, which had a three-digit lock. I set it next to my mom's and went to sleep.

When we arrived in Sudan, I shut the door to my room and opened my suitcase. I moved the clothes out of the way. The packs were unmarked. I snuck up to the roof of the house and tucked them into the empty storage unit. *Nobody uses this thing anyway*, I thought. I locked the door.

DESTINED TO FAIL

THE BRIBE

My dad could outwit you in debate and petrify you in his silences. He was a brilliant man; his memory held the history of the world. He could tell you about the lineage of the Ottoman sultans, remember the exact date of an ancient war, or list off the contents of Lincoln's pockets the night he was assassinated. My dad knew the effect he had on people, and it made him powerful. Others listened when he spoke. He was tough and hardened. In our culture, the family is hierarchical, and the father is considered the god. In this role, he was formidable.

My father had been through several years of university. He saw my lack of interest in school and reiterated his disappointment in me. The lectures were long-winded and given on a regular basis, prompted by my failures to deliver.

I could predict his talking points. *You need to study. Your grades need to go up, so you can get into a good university. You need to do something good with your life.* My eldest sister, Suhair, was bound for medical school. My older siblings were all on paths to success, but she was the most promising. "You should really be more like Suhair," my father liked to say.

My father (center) at work

I didn't excel at the Egyptian private school, and I never did well on tests, which made me nervous. Studying was something I wanted nothing to do with, and an exam only added to the grief. This was the reason my dad yelled at me and insisted on turning any conversation into a lecture. When the only sound in the classroom was the scratch of pencils, I heard his voice. I was sure I'd be reprimanded; I expected the lousy grades.

When school began again, exams arrived too soon. The teacher handed back the first test of the semester, and I saw

DESTINED TO FAIL

the seventy-five. *Passable,* I thought. *But this teacher is my best bet to haggle.*

When my classmates filed out the door, I stayed behind. The teacher brooded behind his desk. *I guess I'm really doing this.* My heart pounded like a mallet.

"Excuse me, sir? I was wondering, if I were to give you a small gift, would you raise my score from a seventy-five to an eighty?"

The teacher shot me a look. *Oh great, this again,* said his expression.

"The seventy-five becomes an eighty," I said. "I'll give you five cigarettes."

The teacher raised his eyebrows then shook off the temptation. "No. That's crazy."

"Are you sure? Jordanian cigarettes are really good," I fibbed. They weren't. "They're hard to come by here."

The teacher said nothing.

"I'll be honest. I'm doing this because I don't want to study. I'll get higher grades, but you'll get some foreign cigarettes. What do you say?"

The teacher furrowed his brow. "All right. I'll take five cigarettes." My teacher crossed out the seventy-five and replaced it with eighty percent. "When can you have those for me?"

"Tomorrow," I said.

The teacher nodded. "Good."

Immensely pleased with myself, I walked to the door. My fingers on the handle, I turned and looked the teacher in the eye. "You can tell the other teachers, too. I'm sure they'd like some foreign cigarettes."

The teachers were all in on it. My cigarettes were more in demand than I'd expected, and the scheme inflated rapidly. I measured the inventory, careful to ensure the bad grade was at least five points higher before I subtracted from the stash. I told no one, not even Mustafa. Others would ruin the fun.

The teachers discussed their deals with me behind closed doors. When I discovered how submissive they were, my study habits loosened. I knew they wouldn't tell my parents or the principal. I figured they didn't want to get fired.

Mustafa and I had become regulars at the military club restaurant. We scaled the fence whenever we fancied something good for dinner. On our sixth visit, we walked in and ordered our usual. The waiter lingered, one eyebrow raised, then turned on his heel and walked briskly through a door in the back.

Mustafa's eyes darted around the room, and he leaned in. "We have a problem. Our parents aren't here."

"Uh, yeah," I scoffed. "Our parents are *never* here."

"No, our parents are *not* here," Mustafa said, gesturing with his head. "Look."

DESTINED TO FAIL

I scanned the restaurant. There was no one white or olive-skinned in sight, except for our table. The room was overwhelmingly Sudanese.

"Crap," I muttered, as the supervisor in military uniform and the waiter marched to our table.

"Where are your parents?" asked the supervisor.

I swallowed. "They dropped us off. They're joining us later."

"We wouldn't have allowed you in without your parents." The supervisor glared.

We fessed up. "We jumped the back fence."

"You're not allowed to do that," said the man in uniform, heatedly. "That's against procedure."

"There is no procedure," I stated. I produced my diplomat card. Mustafa followed.

The man in uniform looked briefly at the cards. "Come with me." He walked Mustafa and me to the gate. "Have a nice day," he said.

When the supervisor was out of earshot, Mustafa and I gasped. We looked at each other and laughed.

"It *works!*" Mustafa exclaimed.

I cackled. "No one can *touch* us!"

We made our way back to our parents. We were still hysterical.

"Let's see what else we can get into with these cards," Mustafa whispered.

Mutual love for anarchy sparked between us. We were gas and fire now.

An anticipated evening at the United Nations in Khartoum kept my mother in front of the bathroom mirror for hours. My parents were due at a United Nations event where President Ahmed al-Mirghani would be in attendance. My dad had stressed its importance, which made my mom wring her hands over what to wear.

I was in my room when I heard my dad's solemn tones from across the house, speaking on the phone with Ali. "You're sure you're too sick to drive?"

They've got no one to drive them to the reception at the UN. I remembered someone telling me ambassadors couldn't drive themselves. *Should I offer to do it for them?* I wanted to help them. I weighed it against my fear of consequence.

My dad hung up the phone and sighed. He said something to my mom, and she made a noise of lament. I walked into the living room, where she sat on the couch, looking worriedly at my dad. I asked what was wrong, pretending I hadn't heard anything.

"We just found out Ali is really sick," she said. "He can't take us to the UN."

"Could you get someone else to take you?" I asked. "Can't dad drive?"

DESTINED TO FAIL

"Ambassadors can't drive. We don't have anyone else," my dad said. He loosened his tie and huffed. "I guess we aren't going."

Dad's gonna whip me with that brown belt. "Dad. I can drive you and Mom. I know how."

My parents stared at me. *Can't take that back now*, I thought. My dad and I locked eyes for thirty years. Something volcanic stirred in his brow, then settled. He made up his mind.

"Go. Get ready. Meet us out front in two minutes."

"What's wrong with you?" my mom hollered.

My dad told her to get in the car, where I sat behind the wheel, atop a stiff pillow. Heart in my throat, I turned the keys in the ignition and pulled onto the road. My mom gasped.

"This isn't happening!" she wailed. "Is our child *driving*?"

My dad gave directions from the backseat. I was wide-eyed and vigilant. In ten minutes, I pulled into the half-moon drive in front of the United Nations. My parents sat in silence for a moment, my mom stunned.

"Your mother and I are going inside," my dad said, his expression severe. "Drive straight home. Be back here in two hours and not a minute later."

My parents entered the gates, where government officials stood to greet them. *I better get outta here before anyone sees*. I slowly meandered out of the half-moon and onto the road, driving by myself for the first time.

Back home, I began to worry. When the time came, I dashed out to the car again. Night had fallen, and my hands were tighter on the wheel. At the UN, my parents were shaking hands with the officials and bidding them farewell. They were silent in the backseat as I drove home. As the house came into view, I braced myself, expecting the worst.

The tension in the living room came from my dad's eyes. They burrowed into mine for a few moments. Perhaps he was trying to glean some information that would not readily slip.

"So," he said. "My chauffeur taught you how to drive. Start from the beginning."

I confessed to haggling with Ali and described how I had been driving regularly. When I finished, my dad spoke again.

"For your age, you're a good driver. We're not angry with you. However, you were unfair to my driver, and that's unacceptable."

I nodded, eyes downcast.

Later, my dad brought it up again. "Since your driving is no longer a secret, I'll let you drive, just not alone. Only when Ali or I are with you."

On weekends thereafter or when Ali was off duty, my dad made a beeline for the passenger's seat.

DESTINED TO FAIL

Driving the embassy car at age 11

As the school year came to a close, football finals began to heat up. I juggled the ball in my yard and conjured glorious outcomes in my imagination. Mustafa, our friends, and I couldn't participate, though: only students ninth grade and up competed. We still wanted to cheer the team on.

During lunch period one day, the students strategized. They wanted to convince the principal to close the school down. Only for three hours though, they conceded. Because this was an away game, they needed to account for travel time plus duration. But no one dared approach the principal, who ruled with fear. The student body sent their legion of goody-two-shoes to appease him.

"Excuse me, sir?" They looked up at him, doe-eyed. "We are here to ask you if you would be so kind to let us leave for a few hours? We want to watch our school play in the final in a few days."

The honors students emerged from the principal's office in defeat. "No luck," they said.

The principal only knew of me because of my formidable father. I'd never had a reason to interact with him. I wasn't a troublemaker, nor was I academically gifted. *What if I talked to him?* I wondered. *If every grown-up here loves my cigarettes so much, why shouldn't the principal? He smokes, too.*

"Why don't I try my luck?" I asked.

"I wouldn't," said one of the honors students. "He seemed mad when we left."

My success rate with the teachers was unparalleled. I shrugged. "I'll be right back."

I walked down the hallway and gently knocked on the door. I heard an invitation to enter. Compared to the light-filled halls, this was the darkest room. A pale beam of light from a sliver of a window caught wisps of cigarette smoke midair and illuminated the principal's sharp chin. The smell of burning rubber hung about him. He looked up at me from his desk.

"Ah, the ambassador's son," the principal said. He shifted forward. His face was hollow and hardened. Arched brows gave him a severity, and bags hung beneath his dark eyes. The principal intertwined his spindly fingers and frowned.

"Mr. Principal, sir," I said. "I was wondering if you could please let us leave for a few hours to watch our school play in the final."

The principal glared. "I already told your friends, and I'll tell you the same thing. *No,* I am not going to do that."

"What if I offered you a small gift in exchange?" I asked.

"What sort of gift?"

"Cigarettes. Imported cigarettes."

The principal's mouth fell open, incredulous. "You're offering me cigarettes? Am I hearing you correctly?"

Instant regret knocked me in the stomach. *What the hell was I thinking?* I pictured the principal calling my dad. I saw my father's rage and winced.

"Yes, I am," I said, feigning confidence. "Cigarettes you won't find here." *I'm screwed anyway,* I thought. *I might as well keep going.*

The principal was silent for a moment. He inhaled. "What kind?"

"They're from Jordan, and they're very good," I said. "Every time a guest at our house smokes one, they always tell us how nice they are."

"How many packs are you offering me?"

"One pack to let us leave for three hours. Once the game is over, we'll be back to finish the last period."

"I would let you all go for five packs," said the principal.

He wants five? Yikes. I couldn't afford to thin out the stash like that.

"Mr. Principal," I said. "There's no way I can get you five packs."

"How many can you give me?"

"I'm going to be honest with you, sir," I said. "I have to steal the cigarettes from my dad's collection, which he keeps for guests in our living room. If five packs are gone, he'll notice. I can snag two, but that's all I can do."

"If you can give me three, we have a deal."

The game was more important than the size of my stash. I smiled, conceding. "I can do that."

"When will you have them for me?" the principal asked.

"The day of. When I leave for the game, I'll stop by your office and drop them off."

"Why can't you bring them tomorrow?"

"What if you change your mind?" I asked.

The principal smiled.

I sprinted back to my friends, grinning.

"Guys, get ready. He's gonna announce it in a second," I said. "He's shutting down the school."

They looked at me and guffawed. "Oh! *Big* man, got the school shut down!" My friends made fun of me until a voice crackled on the PA system and echoed throughout the building. They looked up and were silent.

DESTINED TO FAIL

"*Attention, students. We will be having a half-day at the end of this week. Classes will be canceled in the afternoon. Any student who wants to watch the game may go.*"

My friends' mockery ceased. They gaped. "How did you *do* that? What did you *say* in there?"

"Oh, *now* you wanna know." Jokingly, I gave them the bird.

I came to school the day of the game with three packs of cigarettes in a paper bag, and left it on the principal's desk. Classes finished early, and some classmates sprinted to the public bus. Mustafa and I walked to the other school. We danced and cheered with a hundred other kids. Our team won, easily. Joined by a throng of students, Mustafa and I sang and danced our way back to school. We found the principal, and swarmed him. We threw our arms around him. "Thank you!" a crowd of children chimed. The principal beamed, high on his newfound popularity.

School let out, and I was off to Jordan again with my mom. A week later, I hung out on the curb with my neighborhood friends. My friend, Hamza, was trying out for the junior pro football club at Petra Stadium.

"I really want someone to go with me to the Cubs tryouts," he said. Nobody showed any desire to join him. Hamza looked at me. "Would you want to come?"

The Cubs were a big deal. *I'm good*, I thought. *But I'm not that good.*

"Yeah," I shrugged, nonchalantly. Hamza was a great player, and expected to make it on the team. I just wanted to play in that stadium. *Whatever happens, happens,* I thought.

On Friday morning, Hamza and I clambered onto the public bus. The usual quarter-to-seven commuters were home, and the day of rest cast a silent blanket over the city. We arrived at Petra Stadium, where sixty boys had gathered. The coach introduced himself as Ibrahim. I recognized him from TV. He was the big, stocky man who had played defense on the national football team. He had recently retired and taken over the youth program. His late thirties had supplied him with a thick, full mustache, hairy forearms, and a round potbelly. I was starstruck. *It's him! He's so good!*

Ibrahim divided the kids into groups. We each received either a white or a blue training jersey with a number on the back; an assistant coach wrote down our last names with the corresponding jersey number. Afterward, we scrimmaged. Once in a while, I'd look over at Ibrahim, but the mustache hid any hint of expression. The whistle signaled the end of the scrimmage, and our coach ordered a seated circle around him. He produced the list. "Stand up when I call your name."

Hamza was first to be called. Ibrahim read off the surnames, and the assumption among the boys became that whoever was called had to go home. The ones who stood let out sighs of disappointment. *Don't call my name,* I thought.

DESTINED TO FAIL

"Afana," called Ibrahim. I stood up, deflated.

At the end of the roll call, one half stood and the other remained on the ground. "Everyone seated," said Ibrahim, "go home."

The sitting ones slumped toward the gate. I looked at Hamza in shock, and we giggled. The other standing boys laughed too. "I thought I was going home," we said to each other.

"None of you are safe," Ibrahim said. Our faces fell. "You'd better work hard, and show up to practice on time."

I played on the Cubs team all summer, on Tuesdays and Friday mornings, and held football scrimmages with my friends. Razi and I played computer games. I bought more packs of cigarettes downtown in twos and threes and smuggled them into my room under my mother's nose. When school became a looming prospect again, I told Coach Ibrahim that I had to leave Jordan for the school year. He was displeased.

"My dad's the Ambassador of Jordan, and we're stationed in Sudan," I said. "I go to school there."

Ibrahim nodded. "Come here as soon as you're back next summer," he said.

I said goodbye to Razi. I delicately cushioned the cargo in my suitcase with socks and T-shirts. Again, we were bound for Sudan.

PUBLIC SCHOOL

Khartoum was submerged in a record flood that summer, and my private school sat near the bank of the Nile. The teachers were held back in Egypt, and the school was closed until the waters receded and the clean-up efforts were finished.

My parents deliberated over what they should do with me. At first, my dad thought they should delay my return to school. Instead, he signed me up at public school. On a tour he took with the principal, my dad saw classrooms packed with students, with capacities of a hundred and fifteen (my private school was twenty-five).

The school couldn't afford to supply students with desks and chairs, the principal said. I would need to bring my own. My dad relayed this information to my mom and me at the dinner table. My mom was shocked.

"One hundred and fifteen students in one class?" She gasped.

"And I have to bring my own chair." I giggled. I loved jokes.

DESTINED TO FAIL

"This is only for a few weeks at most. How bad can it be?" my dad said. "It'll go by fast, and you'll be back to your school in no time."

I realized my dad wasn't kidding. I started to worry. "What about Mustafa? Is he coming, too?"

"No, Mustafa isn't back in Sudan yet. His father extended their vacation for a few weeks because of the flood."

My stomach dropped. "Weren't you warned when we first got to Sudan never to consider public schools?"

"The subject is closed for discussion," said my dad.

I hadn't worn a uniform since attending school in Jordan when I was little. On my first day at Sudanese public school, I put on the brown khaki shorts and white button-up shirt everyone else wore, thinking, *I couldn't possibly look more ridiculous.*

"Listen to me, Anas," said Ali, as he pulled up to the building. "I'm not going to lie to you—this is a tough place. Don't get in a fight with anyone, no matter what they say. Public schools in Sudan are brutal. Teachers beat students with whatever they can get their hands on. Keep your mouth shut. Listen to what the teachers say, and never talk back. Got it?"

I peered out the window. "Got it."

"Yesterday, I brought a chair and a small desk to your classroom, as your father ordered. I wrote your name on it so you'll know which one is yours," he added. I nodded and got out of the car.

"Go to classroom 8C."

I shut the car door and started walking. The teasing was immediate.

"Are you lost?"

"Are you sure you're at the right school?"

Ali's words echoed: *keep your mouth shut*. I smiled and kept walking.

The school's interior was peeling and crumbled. The walls of 8C, a ground-floor classroom, were scuffed and marked and had yellowed with age. Three windows on either side let in the fearsome morning sun. The number of students packed into the single room could have equaled the entirety of my old school. Upon my entrance, the class fell still.

"That's him," called one student. "That's the diplomat's son."

"*Halabi!*" they cried, which closely translates to "milky." A cacophony of taunts erupted. Aware of my olive skin and anxious, I silently walked to the middle of the front row. I approached one of the few students who were quiet.

"Do you know where my seat is?"

"Right there, directly behind me," he pointed. "Four rows back."

DESTINED TO FAIL

I spotted my desk and chair. The kids were squeezed together with barely enough room to fidget. There were no aisles. "How do I get there?" I asked.

The boy smiled. "You gotta climb on top of my desk and walk over those other kids' desks till you get to yours."

Here goes nothing. I leapt onto the boy's desk in the front row, and walked over four others' until I reached my own. I breathed when the two boys next to me didn't tease. I stuffed my bag under the desk.

"Just ignore those mean boys," one of them whispered. "They do this to everyone. It's not just you."

"What were they saying?" I asked, grinning. "I was too busy asking directions for the trip to my seat."

The boys laughed. The bell rang. The teacher walked in with a stick of bamboo snug in his right palm. Everyone stood up. I sprang up with them.

The students were ordered to sit. The teacher scanned the room and singled out the milky one. "You. Stand up," he ordered.

I obeyed.

"Where are you from?" the teacher asked.

"Jordan," I said.

"I don't care what you're doing in Sudan. You're in my classroom now. Behave and do your homework, or I will whip you with this stick. Understood?"

"Yes, sir."

"Sit down."

The teacher spoke for the next forty-five minutes. I put my head down and took diligent notes. *This is* not *private school,* I thought. *I have to study.* When class ended, the teacher pointed to a student and beckoned him forward.

"Anyone who speaks before the next teacher arrives or causes a disturbance, write their names on the chalkboard." The teacher handed the boy a piece of chalk.

"Yes, sir," said the boy. The teacher left.

I looked around. The classroom was mostly still. The air had grown thicker. Beads of sweat gathered on the backs of the necks in front of me. In my periphery, I saw two boys speak to each other in soft tones. Their whispers carried over to the front of the room, where the chalk squeaked out their names on the peeling, splintered blackboard.

"*Pssst*! *Halabi!*" I heard some kids call out. I knew they were trying to get me written up, but I kept my head down until the bell rang.

Everyone hushed as the next teacher walked in. He held the short end of a garden hose in his right hand. The teacher dismissed the scribe at the front of the classroom. He traced a finger across the names on the blackboard then over to the two boys who'd been talking. His index finger turned to a hook.

Heads downcast, the boys climbed over the desks to the front. The teacher made a motion with his hand for them to turn around. The stagnant air parted as he raised the end of the hose. With tremendous force, he whacked the student's behind. I almost gasped. The boy's face screwed up in pain, stifling a whimper, as he braced for a second blow. When it arrived, he made no sound. He was ordered back to his desk.

When the second boy was whacked, he let out a scream. The class howled with laughter. Whimpering in pain, the kid struggled to get into position for his second whooping. The teacher grew frustrated and instructed two students in the front row to pull his arms toward them. The hose came down twice as hard. My eyes went wide. *I'm gonna get really good grades.*

At the end of the day, Ali came to pick me up, and I was grateful for the sanctity of the backseat. Still in shock, I told him about the physical abuse I'd watched my classmates endure.

Back home, my mom was waiting for me. "How was school?" she asked with concern.

"It was fine." I smiled. "Not as bad as we were told."

"Really? Are you sure?"

"Yeah," I lied. I didn't want her to worry. "Everything will be fine. Like Dad said, it's just a week or two."

My dad was the authority. I didn't want to go back, but he would only dismiss my protests.

The next few weeks were more of the same. The class was sweaty and packed tight. Raucous laughter erupted as a few students were whipped every day. The taunts continued, and I fought to keep my mouth shut, wishing this time away.

At public school, I was a model student. My grades were exemplary, fueled by rigorous study habits and scrupulous note-taking. It all stemmed from the fear knocked into me every day. To be silent and inconspicuous was my best weapon.

At the beginning of the third week, I ate lunch with the boy next to me. We had slowly become friends.

"It's going to be a long year for you, with those kids calling you names," the boy said.

I hadn't dared to tell anyone that my time here was temporary. *This guy seems all right,* I thought.

"I'm not worried," I said, quietly. "Honestly, I won't be here much longer."

"What do you mean?" the boy asked.

"Don't tell anyone," I said. "My school flooded. I'm just here till it opens again. My dad says they're starting class again next week. I have a few days left here, then I'm going back to my old school."

He sighed. "Lucky you."

"Yeah," I said. "It's been pretty rough here. Watching those kids get whipped is still crazy to me."

The last day of the week rolled around, and relief set in as I walked into school and found my way to 8C. Something had shifted in the classroom, but I couldn't put a finger on it. I walked over the desks as the kids hurled their usual taunts and sat down.

When first period ended, the teacher left. I took out another book from my bag for the upcoming period and started to read the material. The second teacher called my name. I thought the driver had come to pick me up early.

"Do I bring my bag with me?"

"No," the teacher said. "Just come here."

I heard snickering from the side of the room. I paid it no heed and stepped over the desks. The teacher's finger flew through the air to the chalkboard, where my name had been etched. My heart stopped. I shook my head.

"I wasn't talking," I said. "I wasn't making any noise."

"Then why is your name on the board?" the teacher asked.

I stared at the scribe, whose name was Osman. "Osman," I said, "you saw me talking?"

Osman looked back at me. He said nothing. I turned to the teacher in indignation, but he motioned for me to turn around. I obeyed; there was no arguing. As I bent over, I looked down. The teacher gripped a two-foot stick of bamboo in his right hand. *I am so screwed,* I thought. I prepared myself.

SMACK! The bamboo brought water to my eyes. I clenched my fists and stomach muscles. I bit into my bottom lip to keep from howling. My skin was light enough to show the blood rush to my cheeks, which made the students roar with laughter. The teacher suppressed a chuckle before raising his arm even higher. The second beating burned.

I was ordered back to my chair. As I climbed over the desks, I thought, *I know why everybody here wears brown khakis. It's in case kids crap themselves after getting whipped. It's camouflage.*

As soon as the period ended and the teacher had walked out of the room, a boy called out to me. "Hey, *halabi!*"

I looked over at him, shocked that this kid would risk what I had just endured.

"Now you'll remember us when you go back to your school!" he called.

I should've kept my mouth shut. I looked over at the boy next to me and realized he had been the rat.

"I'm sorry," he whispered immediately, brow furrowed in remorse. "I didn't realize they were going to do that."

I was angry, mostly at myself for trusting anyone there. I didn't utter another word to the boy next to me. *Mustafa would never sell me out like that.* The bell rang. I booked it to the car, pursued by taunts, and threw myself onto the backseat, shutting the door tight.

"What's wrong?" Ali asked.

"Nothing. Just drive."

"What about your desk and chair?"

"Drive!" I shouted. "They can have it. I don't want that stupid chair."

DESTINED TO FAIL

Ali pulled onto the road and didn't speak. At home, I heard that Mustafa was back in Sudan. *Boy, do I have some stories for him*, I thought.

After three weeks surrounded by bullies, I was relieved to see Mustafa again and tell him about being whipped at school. Soon, I was back to playing football in the sun with my friends. There were no regimented games, only rowdy scrimmages, but we could go on for hours. Coach Ibrahim's encouragement still buzzed in my head. I was a better player than a lot of my friends. *I'm really good at this*, I thought.

At school, my study habits relaxed without the threat of a beating. For every C-, I let a few cigarettes slip to a teacher, and the grade appeared more agreeable. The year sailed by, and once school let out, Mom and I made arrangements to fly back to Jordan in the coming weeks.

A fan faintly whirred in the late-June heat. I awoke at two in the morning to the growl of military trucks. Several went by, while, outside, a loudspeaker blared. *"Attention, citizens! Do not leave your homes. Anyone who does will be shot on sight."*

I sat bolt upright and was still for a moment, listening. I got out of bed and peered through the curtains.

The recording came from a megaphone atop a military truck. The threats of death receded as the vehicle barreled down the street. Army Jeeps followed, fast and crude, bearing guns and gun turrets pointed in every direction.

Their headlights moved over my neighbors' houses as people looked out their windows, bewildered.

The door to my room flew open, and my mom turned on the lights. She rushed over and threw her arms around me. We drew away from the window. Military helicopters drummed the air above us, and searchlights probed our neighborhood, running along our windows and roof.

My dad joined us. "Sounds like a coup," he said, matter-of-factly.

The Jeeps and helicopters silenced within the hour. We turned on the TV, where a stiff general read from a teleprompter. "*The Rescue Revolution has taken over. We advise you to stay home.*"

Omar al-Bashir's transitional government announced a curfew. Anyone out between 10 p.m. and 5 a.m. were to be shot to death. The airports closed. The embassies in Khartoum received a fax, and my dad was briefed on the event. Army Jeeps, trucks, and tanks paraded the central streets and highways. At night, a checkpoint appeared in our neighborhood, but military presence was relatively sparse. The government hardly bothered with the embassy neighborhood.

I stayed close to home. A week later, the airports reopened, and my mom and I were on the first flight out to Jordan for the summer.

Back in Amman, without a thought to unpacking my suitcase, I hopped on a public bus. At the club house, I asked

DESTINED TO FAIL

for Coach Ibrahim. I was directed across the street to the complex of courts and stadiums.

At Petra Stadium, Ibrahim was running practice. He remembered me but had forgotten my name. "You're the ambassador's son, right?"

He told me to show up on Friday at eight o'clock sharp.

I was present for every practice. A few weeks into the season, Ibrahim announced we would compete with another Cubs team from across town.

On the day of the game, we were each given a crisp, blue uniform. I held mine in disbelief. *Wow! An official Cubs jersey!* I put it on and felt like an action hero in cleats. I was number nine.

I sat on the bench for the entirety of the first half. I clapped when my teammates scored. Then, at halftime, Ibrahim called my number.

"Afana," he said, "you're going in."

I assumed my position as a Left Forward and breathed to steady my heart. The whistle sounded, and I jumped into a run. The ball zipped from the opposition to my teammates. An attacker on my team set me up, and I had possession of the ball. One defender from the opposition barreled toward me, then another. My feet outwitted them.

There were a few instances when I might have scored, but the goalie sailed in front of the ball and prevented it. Then, in a split second, space and time were in my favor. A window opened, and I kicked the ball with all the force in my calves.

My team went wild. I couldn't comprehend it. *Did I just score my first goal?* I looked around, excited, at my teammates, who slapped me on the back. I felt possessed by something wonderfully addictive, and I wanted another.

I scored the next goal, and it brought the game to 4-2. I ascended into the high. *Surely this is a dream.* My teammate scored the last goal, and we won 5-2. In the club house, the team was triumphant.

"You all played well," Ibrahim said over the din of our celebration. "But you still need to improve. Next week, we'll be playing against a much better team."

I gathered my things, slung a bag over my shoulder, and made my way out of the club house.

"*Afana!*"

I turned to see Ibrahim's face furrowed in approval. He gave me a thumbs-up.

I grinned the whole bus ride home. *I scored two goals. And Coach Ibrahim really likes me.* I felt a rush of confidence. *If he thinks I'm really good, it must be true.*

The tough team came a week later. We maintained a dynamic back-and-forth game. I scored one goal, and my teammates scored the others. We tied, 3-3.

That season, our team almost kept a winner's streak. The only loss was 1-0. In every game, I scored at least once.

DESTINED TO FAIL

Each time, Coach Ibrahim gave me seeds of encouragement. At the end of the summer, I announced my departure.

"As soon as you're back in Jordan," Ibrahim said, "I want you to come and see me. I have big plans for you."

"Yes, sir," I said.

"Keep practicing," he insisted. "I want to see you better next year. You hear me?"

"Yes, sir," I said. "I'll definitely practice. We play a lot of football in Sudan."

ANAS AFANA & STELLA BELLOW

HITCHHIKERS

After Omar al-Bashir's coup, Khartoum gleamed. The garbage on the street had vanished. Buses and cars cruised down new streets, free of potholes. The aroma of fresh paint hung thick in the air. Electricity was more reliable, gas tanks were full, and sugar was in abundance. People were fearful yet pacified. The riots had ceased.

When the Brigadier General gained enough power, the curfew was lifted. In August, when my mom and I returned from Jordan, I went back to school and played with my friends again. In spite of the political turmoil, I loved the Sudanese people, who were kinder and more generous than any place I had been. Things were safer in Khartoum than in Paris when we had lived there; aside from the riots and upheaval, we never heard of or encountered any crime. In 1989, the country in the grip of totalitarianism didn't look much different to me than before. To a kid, politics were inconsequential.

DESTINED TO FAIL

I got in the car one day after school, and instead of taking the way home, Ali took Nile Street. Often, I sat here by the river with my friends.

"Where are we going?" I asked.

"Picking up your dad at the Presidential Palace," Ali said.

Outside, I watched the square buildings lining the road turn to palm trees. Sunlight dappled the pavement where African tulip trees wove leafy tents over the road. Light bounced off the river. When his turn signal clicked, Ali turned off Nile Street, and the car rolled along a white pronged fence until we reached a gate. The Jordanian flag on our car's fender told the guard we were welcome, and the gates swung open.

We rolled up to the back entrance of the palace. There were staircases with sweeping handrails, battlements, and arched entries, all blindingly white. Pruned hedges stood sentinel at the base of the stairwells, and regal palms waved their long fronds. I was in awe and decided to walk around.

After the chauffeur parked, I strolled the grounds and gazed up at the white fortress. A guard noticed I was unaccompanied.

"Who are you here with?" he asked.

"I'm just waiting for my dad," I said. "He's the ambassador of Jordan."

"Oh." The guard nodded then pointed me down a path. "You should go that way, to the little kitchen. There's a guy there named Mansur. Tell him I sent you."

I thanked him and walked toward an extension of the palace that resembled a small, neat house. The smell of cooked fish wafted out to the gardens. A friendly and gregarious man named Mansur greeted me. I introduced myself, and he ushered me in.

"What can I get you? Orange juice? Mango juice? A fish sandwich?"

"All of it!" I exclaimed.

Oil sizzled behind Mansur as he asked me where I was from. I told him, and he said he'd love to visit someday. A filet of tilapia dropped into a skillet. I received the second course, a glass of mango juice, which was thick and sweet. Then, Mansur presented me with a crisp, juicy fish sandwich. I devoured it and thanked him.

"Don't mention it," he said. "Hope to see you again sometime."

I walked back to the car and waited for my dad in the backseat. A few minutes later, I saw his head appear at the top of the stairs. His torso and legs followed, and he beckoned. I got out of the car and walked up the white steps. The head of a second figure came into view. I reached the top step, vaguely recognizing the other man. A white jalabiya was draped over the moon of his potbelly.

"This is my son," said my dad.

DESTINED TO FAIL

The man attempted a smile, despite his customary frown. He shook my hand with one broad palm and patted me on the head with the other. I felt the giant, bedazzled band on his ring finger knock against my scalp. Then, the men politely bid each other farewell.

"I look forward to working with you," my dad said, and I followed him down the stairs. When I turned back, I saw the man disappear through a door.

In the car, I asked my dad, "Who was that?"

"That was the president," he said. "Omar al-Bashir."

My eyes opened wide. Every man in Khartoum wore a jalabiya, and the person I'd just met seemed as ordinary as anybody on the street. But he was the president. *I just ate fish sandwiches,* I thought, *at his house.*

My dad was connected to all sorts of prominent figures. Princess Wijdan, the cousin of King Hussein, visited us in Khartoum with her daughter, Princess Basma. Wijdan was kind, and her daughter and I got along. At the time, the violence in Sudan was concentrated in the south, where a civil war was ongoing.

When my dad and Princess Wijdan had finished whatever business they had to discuss, she asked, "Could we go south to Al Dinder, on a safari trip?"

From right to left, Princess Wijdan with her arm around me, the wife of a Sudanese official, and Wijdan's daughter, Princess Basma

Two army helicopters flew us to Dinder National Park in the south. Princess Wijdan, Princess Basma, my parents, and I were in one, while the other barreled ahead of us. The ground was festooned in tufted trees and grasslands.

The first chopper landed before us and disgorged a militia of soldiers armed with machine guns. When our chopper landed, we were led to round tents made of sturdy grasses, like gazebos, with no doors.

On the safari, we saw zebras, giraffes, and gazelles. They grazed peacefully or perked up their sensitive ears to sense any lurking predator. We heard the lions from far off but never saw one. Monkeys flew from the thick tree branches. At night, a soldier sat watch by my bed with a machine gun. I couldn't sleep.

On another trip with my parents, in 1989, I stood on a rickety steamship that inched along the Nile. By the banks, women washed their clothes. People in the nude plunged into the water and scrubbed themselves clean. In the distance, I saw a remote island, which I asked about from below deck.

Discovering Crocodile Island

"It's well known among the locals, the villagers of Altekaina," said the captain. "Fishermen come here often."

In the distance, I saw the fishermen in loose, billowing shirts and jalabiyas. They balanced in canoes and cast their nets in full motions. The shores of the island were fine and white, uncommon on the banks of the Nile. A bright, green forest grew at the center, resembling the gnarled spine of a crocodile emerging from the water.

I conjured fantasies of secret trips to the crocodile island. Over the next few weeks, I gathered my accomplices. "There's this island on the Nile," I said. "It's got white sandy beaches, and it's right off the highway, an hour from Khartoum."

My friends were eager, and we discussed travel plans in an official meeting. We eliminated our parents' help from the equation immediately.

"They would never allow us an hour away," we agreed. "Especially to some island in the middle of nowhere."

After factoring in logistics—like time, weather, transportation—we formed a mission. My friends and I would wake up early and walk to the highway. After an hour in someone's car, we would reach the village and ask a fisherman to row us across the river. At the end of the day, we would find another fisherman, walk to the highway, and hitchhike back to Khartoum. To us, the plan was foolproof. We arranged to meet early one morning at one of my friends' houses down the street. From there, we'd depart on our runaway picnic.

"I'm waking up early tomorrow morning for a football tournament," I announced to my mom. This was my diversion, so she wouldn't worry.

I awoke in the dark. Full of energy, I dressed, scarfed down some breakfast, and walked to my friend's house. Everyone brought assorted fruits and vegetables for lunch. One of my friends carried a football. We walked along the main highway by the airport as the sun rose. We waved down a truck to hitch a ride.

The driver noticed us and pulled over. Good-naturedly, he asked, "What are you kids doing here so early?"

"We'd like you to give us a lift, near Altekaina, please," we replied.

"Get in the back," he said.

The trip took an hour. The driver offered to take us there for free, since his route was straight down the highway anyway. A few of my friends dozed off in the early morning. I couldn't sleep; it was too hot and windy. When the truck stopped to let us out, my friends and I gave the driver ten pounds in appreciation. He smiled and thanked us.

"There's an island near the village that we're looking for," I said. "How would we get there?"

"Walk that way for about twenty minutes." The driver pointed. "Then, you'll reach the river."

The sun grew warmer as we walked through the desert. The sand was still cool on our feet. On the shore of the Nile, my friends and I scouted the water for a fisherman. As we waited, a boy from Altekaina came into view, leading a speckled donkey. A friend of mine approached him.

"Hey," he said, "would you let us take rides? We'll give you a pound per person."

"Sure," said the boy.

My friend saddled up and rode the donkey in circles, while someone stood watch by the water for a fisherman. Finally, one came into view, and we flagged him down. He rowed toward us in a long, wooden canoe.

My friends and I explained where we wanted to go and offered to pay him. He demanded an astronomical price. I was the negotiator of the group and made several attempts to lower the number. The fisherman was stubborn.

"I'm not taking you kids across the river for anything less than forty pounds," he said.

"Forty pounds is ridiculous. This isn't our first time," I lied. "I'll pay you twenty, and that's my final offer. If you don't take it, we'll wait for someone else. It's still early, and we're not in a rush."

One of my friends rides a donkey

In the canoe, rowing towards Crocodile Island

The fisherman raised his brows over sun-strained eyes.

"Deal," he said. He helped us with our food and belongings as we boarded his canoe. The fisherman was broad-shouldered and rowed us across the Nile with fearsome biceps.

On the shores of the island, we unloaded the food. I had bought a fish to grill. We thanked the fisherman, and I handed him the money before we waved him goodbye.

My friends and I played a game of football on the cool sand in the morning. Then, we collected dry sticks, built a fire, and grilled the fisherman's kill, which we ate with fruit. My friends and I picked at the tender fish, making sounds of satisfaction. When football in the heat became unbearable, we splashed into the water. We kicked off our shoes and played where it was shallow or swam in the deep end.

As we dried off in the sun, I looked around. My friends were sprawled about—a ball under an arm, a slice of watermelon dripping between someone's fingers. We were alone and unsupervised on an island in the middle of the Nile. I could have stayed there forever.

In the afternoon, we scouted for a few minutes to spot a fisherman. The horizon had emptied of canoes, and we realized fishermen were more common in the mornings than the afternoons. We started to panic.

"It's getting late," one friend said. "And we still have to hitchhike home."

DESTINED TO FAIL

"What if no one shows up?" asked another. The question hung unanswered. For thirty minutes, we watched the water in fretful silence. I wished I could see all the way up the river.

"I see one!" someone hollered.

The fisherman had already spotted us and was rowing toward the island. My friends and I gathered together and waved. I asked if he could row us to shore.

"Sure thing," said the fisherman. We clambered aboard and thanked him profusely on the other side of the river. We gave him ten pounds as a token of our gratitude. He smiled and rowed away.

My friends and I regrouped. The idea was to run back to the highway, but we all felt one another's exhaustion. We had been awake since five in the morning then had run around and kicked a ball, swam in the river, and baked in the sun.

Our pace slowed as we walked through the desert toward the main road. The sand burned our feet. On the side of the road, my friends and I threw up the hitchhiking sign. Almost immediately, a rusty Toyota pickup truck pulled over, curious as to what five olive-skinned boys were doing on the side of the highway.

"Could we get a ride to Khartoum?" we asked.

The driver pointed to the bed of the truck. "Hop in."

During another hour on the highway, exhaustion knocked us asleep on the ride home. One friend jerked awake.

"Guys, we can't *all* sleep," he said.

Two of us pried our eyes open and sat vigil. We arrived unharmed back in the capital city and split ways. My parents suspected nothing.

My friends and I had executed two successful missions to Crocodile Island before I invited Mustafa. He was the more cautious of the bunch, but I still wanted my best friend to come.

"Hey, Mustafa," I began. "You should come to Crocodile Island with me and my friends sometime. It's the best."

Mustafa shook his head. "I'm not going with you. We've done some crazy things, and I've had fun. But leaving Khartoum to go to some island super-far away? That's where I draw the line."

"Why not?" I asked. "It's not that far from Khartoum. We've been there twice, and nothing's happened. Everyone was really helpful and nice."

"Maybe," Mustafa answered. "But my dad would kill me if he found out I was somewhere outside Khartoum. You can do whatever you want, but I can't risk it."

I didn't push Mustafa any further. We both had strict fathers; my dad would kill me, too. Mustafa and I had different thresholds for thrill seeking: we both feared consequence, but I had a higher tolerance for risk. I had already escaped punishment for the driving and still managed to keep the cigarette operation a secret. Mustafa had more to lose.

The Runaway Picnics continued throughout the school year of 1990. We brought cameras and boomboxes and never left without a football. On one trip, my friend rolled up the rug from his kitchen and brought it along, so we wouldn't have to burn ourselves on the hot sand during our picnic. We made fun of him until lunchtime, when the bottoms of our feet burned.

"That carpet was a *brilliant* move," we said.

Most fishermen and truck drivers we met were unassuming and generous. They seldom asked for money, only gestured to the back and said, "Get in." When one asked for money, I did the haggling. Where my North African friends spoke French among themselves, I was fluent in the Sudanese dialect.

"Anas, talk to this guy about money," they would say with a laugh. "You're so good at it!"

I developed a system with the fishermen. After the scare of the first day, I figured the return trip had more value. The agreed price usually came to thirty pounds. I paid ten up front and offered twenty as an incentive to return. The fishermen always came back.

Friend with our picnic rug

One day, I sat with my friend, Ihab, on the stretch of the Nile nearby where the palace stood. A cargo ship sailed past as we heard a commotion of engines behind us. Sleek black cars with flags on their fenders filed into the gates of the palace. I looked at Ihab.

"The car's right there," I said. "Why don't we sneak in and get some free orange juice? I know someone in there."

Ihab was incredulous. "Sneak into *where*?"

"Yeah," I said. I looked at Ali. "Put the flag up. Let's just go in with those other cars."

"Are you crazy?" Ali said. "No. We'd have to be picking up the ambassador for the flag to go up."

"Guys," I said, "it'll work. Trust me. We'll put the flag up, follow the cars, and pretend we're picking up my dad."

"I don't know why I listen to you," said Ali.

"Because you like adventure, too," I said. "And I tip you."

Ali caved. "Fine. Let's go."

The car approached the entrance. "We're here to pick up my father," I said, and the gates opened immediately.

Ihab gaped. "I can't believe that worked."

Ali parked in front of the palace. We strolled the grounds and greeted the guards like we belonged. One of them stopped us and asked where we were going.

"We're going to see Mansur with the juice," I said. "My dad's inside, and we're bored."

We walked over to the extended kitchen, where I introduced Mansur to Ihab. We washed down more fish sandwiches with orange and mango juice. Content and well-fed, we thanked him. Mansur gave us another sandwich for the road and told us to come again.

Ihab and I walked over the grounds unquestioned. I gave the extra sandwich to Ali.

On the drive home, Ihab was thrilled. "I can't believe we just broke into the Presidential Palace!"

"I can," Ali said with a groan. "This kid comes up with ridiculous stuff all the time."

One of the members of the Runaway Picnics was my Libyan friend, Husam. He was the devil, an instigator of mischief far worse than I. The only reason I justified spending time with him was that he was a good football player, and I liked him on my team.

We were walking through the embassy neighborhood in Khartoum one day, to our Algerian friend's house a few streets over. Thick trees with feathery tops provided areas of shade by the embassy entrances, where the Sudanese guards took fortifying naps after lunch.

Husam and I passed the embassy of the Soviet Union, where a girthy tree stood outside. Two guards napped on one side of the trunk, and an army Jeep was parked on the other in the shade, where the steering wheel wouldn't heat up in the sun. I remembered bribing the guards of the Jordanian embassy with cigarettes to drive around in one of their army Jeeps.

"I know how to drive one of those," I remarked, absent-mindedly.

"Really?" Husam asked. "How?"

"I asked the guards nicely, and they let me," I said. No one could know about the cigarette scheme, especially this kid. "Those Jeeps don't require keys or anything."

Husam's eyes gleamed. "What if we just kinda steal it?"

"*No*, we're not *stealing* the Jeep!" I said. "Are you kidding?"

"We'll only steal it for a little while," he said. "Come on. It'll be fun."

DESTINED TO FAIL

Somehow, Husam talked me into it. The doors of the Jeep were big and riddled with battle wounds, prone to creaking and slamming. Carefully, I prised the driver's side open, and Husam sat shotgun.

I started the car and put it in reverse. We flew backward. The guards sprang up, and their mouths fell open. I cleared the tree, put it in first gear, and floored it.

The guards hollered, chasing us halfway down the street until I picked up speed. They clutched their sides, out of breath, as I turned the corner. Husam and I laughed and shouted, and Husam drummed on the dashboard.

When he turned to look back and cackle at the guards, his face froze. "We have all their ammo," he said.

I glanced in the rearview. The back of the Jeep was piled with machine guns and bullet belts. We looked at each other, stunned.

"That's how we didn't get shot," I said. We broke into laughter.

I made right turns until we were back at the Soviet Union embassy, where the guards shook their fists and chased us, angrier than before. I cut a right corner again and chased them in a circle around the block. The guards were exhausted and furious. I was laughing, while Husam was in diabolical ecstasy.

"*Faster!*" he shouted.

The military Jeep flew down the street. The guards only chased us so far. We went for a joyride with the windows rolled down. I turned up sand, doing doughnuts. Red desert cascaded off the bulletproof windshield.

Then, the roar of the motor suddenly made me come to my senses. I glanced at the fuel gauge and hit the brakes.

"We're gonna run out of gas," I said. "We've gotta go back." Husam deflated.

As we approached the embassy, we saw that a few guards had their machine guns out. Husam stuck his whole torso out the window and waved in irreverence. The guards from the other embassies on the block had heard about the stolen Jeep, and an army of twenty waited for us.

Husam pulled his body back into the vehicle. I parked behind the tree. We rolled up our windows and made sure the doors were locked. Several guards came over and jerked the handle on the driver's side.

"Get out of the car!" they barked.

I put up my index finger: *one second*. I reached into my pocket. Husam did the same and took out the diplomat card his father had given him. I pressed my card to the window. I kept from laughing as the crowd of guards scrunched their noses and stuck out their necks to read.

Cannot be arrested, they mouthed. "Okay." They nodded. "Just get out."

As soon as I opened the door, they crowded me and shouted.

"Back up!" I said, shooing them away. "I need room!"

"You stole the car!"

"It's not stealing if you bring it back."

"I'm telling your dad!"

I shook my head. "I know you're not. This is a good lesson for you, not to sleep under trees at work."

Husam and I walked, untouched, through the army of embassy guards and continued on to our friend's house down the street.

The summer I turned fourteen, I continued the cigarette scheme. I played with the Cubs, where Coach Ibrahim told me I got better every year. The Iraqi invasion of Kuwait murmured on our television. When I returned to Khartoum with my mom, overflowing with cigarettes, more Middle Eastern countries had joined the conflict. I overheard my dad's conversation with a colleague from the embassy.

"Jordan will never be the same. With King Hussein being the pacifist he is, Iraqi refugees will flock to the open borders. This won't be a quick fix. It's the beginning of the end for the Middle East."

Life had changed drastically for Mustafa. He didn't talk about it; none of the Iraqis did. But a guard was always beside him when he walked into school. He wasn't allowed in the yard on his own. I could only visit Mustafa at his house, if I wanted to see him; the minute the last class of the day let out, he had to go home immediately.

In January 1991, I watched the first bombs drop on Iraq and Kuwait. A few days into the start of the war, I received a phone call. It was Mustafa, who told me he was leaving Sudan.

"You're leaving?"

I sank into a chair and clutched the receiver. It began to make sense. The Gulf War. How turbulent things were, for Iraqis in particular. How unsafe Mustafa was.

"Where are you going?" I asked.

"My dad told me I can't tell you," Mustafa said. I heard the misery in his voice. "Mom and I are taking the next flight out tomorrow. We're going somewhere safe. Dad told me you and your parents can come to see us off in the morning."

"Is this goodbye?" My voice wavered. My first best friend was leaving me.

"Yeah," he replied, sounding somber. "I'm really sorry about this, man. I'll see you tomorrow."

Mustafa hung up, and the dial tone rang in my ears. My heart broke as I hung up the phone and sat alone in the living room. I felt for Mustafa, who must have been as sad to leave as I was to see him go.

The next day, my parents and I drove to the airport to see Mustafa and his mother off. Our mothers had been good friends. My parents bid the Iraqis farewell and left. I stayed behind. Mustafa and I stood on the tarmac, and I gave him my addresses, in Jordan and in Sudan.

"There's no point in me giving you my Iraqi one," Mustafa said. "We're never going back. But I'll write you."

DESTINED TO FAIL

I looked my friend in the eye for the last moment I would ever see him. I stood with his father as Mustafa followed his mother up the stairs. The plane closed its doors and took off. I waved until I couldn't see the plane anymore.

Mustafa's father gave me a ride home. From the silence, he could tell I was trying not to cry. When the car pulled up in front of the house, he hugged me. "Thank you for being a good friend to Mustafa," he said.

I got inside and closed the door. When I saw my mom, I burst into tears.

The nomadic lifestyle was one of heartache. Life was full of goodbyes: they took place in France, in Jordan, in Sudan. Wherever I went, all my friendships had an expiration date. Mustafa was the most important one. I felt the loss in a pit in my stomach that only widened.

I descended further into misery as the truth became more apparent: I would never see Mustafa again. The ensuing months were dismal. The letter he promised never arrived. I was lonely.

Through football, I eluded sadness. I had an affinity with the other bodies who ran with me, and the current in my legs made endorphins rush in. I practiced for when I would see Ibrahim again. I was happiest there.

The cigarette operation continued to thrive. They were gifts to my teachers on holidays. I pretended to study when my parents watched. I was half-studying when my dad came into my room one night. I hurriedly opened a textbook and pretended to look up from reading.

"What's going on, Dad?" I asked.

He rifled through some of my books. "I know you have exams coming up, and I wanted to test your knowledge."

My heart sank. "Go ahead," I said. "Ask away."

My dad asked a fleet of questions that caught me off guard. His mere presence made my mind freeze. I hadn't studied any of it: math, science, history. The subjects became more rudimentary.

"How do you calculate the area of a triangle?"

I didn't remember.

"What's photosynthesis?"

I looked at the floor. My dad inhaled sharply.

"How are you doing on your tests?"

"Fine," I told him. "I've been getting As and Bs so far."

"If you're passing your tests, why couldn't you answer my questions? What's going on?"

"Nothing," I replied. "I'm just tired. I might need a refresher on certain subjects."

My dad saw through me. "I'm coming to school with you tomorrow," he said coldly. "I'm going to get to the bottom of this. Either something is wrong with that school or something is up with you. And I have a feeling it's the latter."

He left the room. I swallowed the air and stared at the floor in dread. Sleep that night was impossible. I kicked

DESTINED TO FAIL

myself. *I should have studied more.* In the early morning, my mind's eye saw the stash of cigarettes in the storage space on the roof. I reassured myself that somehow everything would turn out all right. I would avoid my academics a little longer. I wouldn't get found out.

The car pulled up to school the next morning, and I bit my nails. My dad walked me down the hall and strode into the principal's office without knocking. The principal was caught off guard. Fear leapt into his eyes at the sight of the ambassador.

"Your Excellency, sir. What brings you here?"

"I'm here to ask about my son's progress in school," said my dad. He sat himself down across from the principal. "I quizzed him last night on several subjects. He couldn't give me answers, even on the basic concepts. Yet I asked him about his test scores, and he told me As and Bs. Can you please explain to me what's going on?"

"Anas is a good student," said the principal. "I don't see what the matter is here."

"Oh, but there is something quite the matter," my dad continued. "It's impossible that my son is passing his classes but cannot answer questions regarding basic academic knowledge."

"I can assure you, Mr. Ambassador, sir, your son is a good student. I like him. The teachers like him, and his friends like him."

"I don't believe you. Anas doesn't know anything. He should be failing, not getting the grades he has."

The air in the office swam with all sorts of creatures. My nerves. The principal's fear. My dad's suspicion. I could have solved the issue for them. But if there was a slim chance I could evade consequence, I'd take it. I studied my shoes while they argued.

Finally, the principal looked at me. "Go to first period, so you won't be late."

For the first time, I was eager to get to class. As I sat at my desk, I spiraled into the dark, anxious corners of my mind. I gazed at the tendril of smoke from a cigarette balanced between the teacher's fingers.

Thirty minutes later, the PA system crackled. *"Anas Afana, return to the principal's office immediately."* My heart dropped. I rose from my seat and slowly walked down the hall. I had built a trap for myself, and the teeth of it closed in further on me. My clammy hand turned the door knob, and I stood, pale-faced, at the threshold. My dad looked grim.

The principal gestured for me to sit.

"Anas, did you bribe your teachers for higher grades?" he asked.

I had no idea how they'd figured it out. I looked at my dad and swallowed. Perhaps the truth would ultimately ease my consequences.

"Yes," I said. "I bribed my teachers with cigarettes."

DESTINED TO FAIL

I felt my dad's eyes sear into the side of my head.

"Which teachers did you bribe?" the principal asked.

"All of them, sir," I replied. *Maybe he'll help me out,* I thought.

My dad never broke his stare. The principal sighed.

"I'm disappointed in you, Anas. What you did was wrong. I assure you, Your Excellency, this will not happen again, and Anas will be punished."

He's trying to save his own skin! I thought. At my age, I knew better than to bribe, but the adults here were corrupt. I was in trouble, anyway. I didn't bother hiding my anger.

"Mr. Principal, why don't you tell my father how I bribed you, *too!*" I exclaimed. "Wasn't it *you* who accepted three cigarette packs from me and agreed to close the school for half a day, so we could all go to the football finals?"

"You too, huh?" asked my dad. He flew out of his seat and towered over the principal. Nuclear rage burst the seams of his stoicism. I had seen this side of my dad before, and I was glad not to be the man behind the desk.

The principal trembled beneath the ambassador like a hunted animal. The color drained from his face. He opened his mouth to defend himself. My dad slammed the desk, and the principal and I flinched.

Dad turned to face me. "Get your things. Meet me by the car."

As I walked back to the classroom, I heard my dad's shouts from the principal's office. We left school early. My dad was livid as the car pulled onto the road. I knew he was itching to lecture me but wouldn't do it in front of the driver. He stared straight ahead. We didn't speak until we were home.

My mom was surprised to see me. "Shouldn't you be in school?"

My dad explained everything. I saw my mom's disappointment through her fury. To disappoint my dad was one thing; it had occurred at a greater frequency. To let my mom down required something really egregious, and I had committed the deed. The remorse stung.

"How long have you been bribing your teachers?" my dad asked.

"I just started this year."

"Where did you get the cigarettes?"

"From around here," I said. "With my allowance."

"Did you smoke any of them?"

"No." I told the truth. "I don't smoke."

My mom shook her head. "I've had enough of this place," she said. "As soon as this school year is over, we're going back to Jordan."

For once, my dad agreed with her. Education was the most important thing to him, and here I was, uneducated. He still pointed out that I needed to transfer schools. They couldn't afford to let me fall further behind.

DESTINED TO FAIL

"How are we going to do that?" my mom said, exasperated. "How is he going to learn a year's worth of knowledge? Where would we transfer him?"

I was too ashamed to tell them that it was not a year's worth but four. Still, my parents launched the plan to get me up to speed on my academics. I transferred to a new school in Khartoum two days later.

My parents hired several tutors. They came in droves and filled me in on the subjects I'd missed. Evasion of responsibility was out of the question now. The adventures were over. My mom sat with me and ensured I was up on all the material. My dad, the encyclopedic one, quizzed me on certain topics. I couldn't complain; I had done myself in.

Part of me wished my dad had made me stay at Sudanese public school. For those few weeks, I was an impeccable student. If I had stayed, I would have been driven to do well out of fear. Now, serious studying was forced on me. My grades improved, and I got Cs on my tests through my own effort. The bribes continued, but the scheme was not as all-encompassing. Just enough to get out of a class or two.

As the school year continued, my parents never discovered the cigarette stash. My dad continued to express his disappointment in me during our interactions, which consisted either of terse sentences that got to the point or outright silence. Our encounters were charged and tense and made me feel guilty. The atmosphere continued long into the spring, as my mom and I prepared to leave for Jordan.

I had bribed my teachers for good grades to make my dad proud, but now he was more displeased with me than ever. I couldn't take the bribery back, but I needed him to understand my remorse. I decided to come clean about the stash. Besides, I had nothing to lose by telling him.

"There's something I need to tell you," I said to my dad. "Remember that thing I said about getting my cigarettes locally? I was lying. I got them all in Jordan."

Dad interrogated me. "Where did you get this idea from?"

"Nobody," I said. "I came up with it myself."

"How many cigarettes are there? Where do you keep them?"

"There are a few left," I answered. "They're in the storage unit on the roof."

"You finish packing. I'll deal with them."

By late May 1991, the low-hanging sun had provoked my mother sufficiently. She was tired of living in this cursed and blistering country. "Stay as long as you need," she said to my father. "Six months, five years, I don't care. We're going home. For good."

As the plane lurched forward on the tarmac, I felt my belly turn over. The faces of the friends I'd made in Sudan came into my mind's eye, and I had some brief memory of

DESTINED TO FAIL

each of them. Crude jokes, stomachs aching with laughter. A football at our toes.

I thought of Mustafa the longest.

The plane lifted. Beneath us, brilliant yellows became shades of golden brown, and I caught a last glimpse of the Nile. My heart hurt for Sudan. I knew I'd never return.

YOU HAVE WHAT IT TAKES

I thought about Coach Ibrahim. *I got so much better at football in Sudan. Now I can really impress him.* This relieved me a little. My classes wouldn't be the point; they never were. I had made up my mind that my devotion was to football alone. The adults lost sleep over my future, but I wasn't worried. The sport waited for me to make a life from it.

My mom and I landed in Cairo for our usual layover. A few hours later, we were on the plane back to Amman. The touchdown was joyful. I watched my mom inhale with satisfaction the Jordanian air. *We're home.* We walked through the terminal and watched for our family.

"Anas!" I heard a voice exclaim. I ran toward the source.

"Razi!" I flung my arms around my cousin. He was taller now but had maintained his dimples, like all the faces on my mom's side of the family. My mom held my sisters close. They were happy to see me.

DESTINED TO FAIL

At home, I became the subject of my parents' concern. They argued about my academic failure over the phone. "How will we save our son?" was the refrain.

My mom rolled up her sleeves and hired tutors to prepare me for the school year. I was overwhelmed with chemistry and physics lessons. My neurons worked overtime. It was difficult for me to sit still.

"You had better take this seriously," the grown-ups admonished. "You have two years left until you graduate. No more horsing around. You need to pass."

At Jordanian school, I quickly realized I was at the bottom of my class. The subjects were rigorous: I went from algebra in Sudan to calculus in Jordan. To understand each concept required entire semesters of material I hadn't paid attention to before. I understood nothing. Words made their way into my ears that my brain couldn't absorb.

In Sudan, I'd been free to achieve my ends by deceit. Even the adults had succumbed to my wiles. The Egyptian teachers had one lazy eye on their students, the other hungrily fixed on a half-finished cigarette. At Jordanian school, though, there was no room for nonsense. The teachers were austere and strong of mind. Their lessons flew over my head. I had to bring all my chemistry work to the tutor. There were so many questions, I wasn't sure where to start.

"What about this problem do you not understand?" the tutor asked.

I shook my head. "The whole thing."

On the first day of school, I knew no one, save for my next-door neighbor. Somehow, we landed in the same class. When I saw him, I breathed easy.

"Amjad!" I called in a loud whisper.

My neighbor turned around. "Anas!"

The two of us walked home together and back to school the next day.

In high school, I wanted to shrink from my classmates. The boys seemed to tower over me, academically advantaged and assertive. They were a year or two older. I was always one of the younger students because, when I was little, my dad enrolled me in school earlier than most Jordanian children. Now, the boys shaved their faces and grew hairs on their meaty knuckles. I assumed a shy persona and sat at the back of the class. If I were absent for a day, no one would miss me. I was an unknown to my teachers, disappearing into the passing average. Ds and the occasional C sufficed.

When my dad returned from Sudan, his appearance had turned more severe. The tuft of hair on his head was taller, and the stark patch of white at its part had risen with it. As he reprimanded me, I fixed my stare on the floor. "Sixty-fives don't put food on the table."

When I came home from school, my dad beat me over the head with math and Arabic grammar. The lectures and nagging became frequent. I avoided him: when I heard him

DESTINED TO FAIL

approaching the kitchen, I scuttled off to my room in the basement. I stayed late at school football practice and made excuses to be elsewhere.

The adults deliberated over possible careers I could pursue. When I was younger and grades were less of an issue, my mom mused that I would be the family dentist. My dad used to counter her.

"Anas is going to study political science. He'll follow in my footsteps and be the ambassador."

As the years passed and my indifference toward school stuck, my parents were less optimistic. The idea of "dental technician" sprang from a conversation between my mom and my cousin. Dental technicians manufactured and repaired prosthetics: false teeth, dentures, and crowns. They had to be dexterous with materials like metal and porcelain.

My cousin was at dental school. Many of the dental technology students were artistic. She saw that I liked to make things with my hands, that I liked to work with wood. She saw the innovative projects I made in the basement. To be a dental technician didn't come with the suffocating amount of study required of a dentist. And, in Jordan, it was respectable.

I laughed at the notion. My mind had been set on professional football. As the people in my world knew, navigating a ball on an open field was my life force.

This time, I could tell Coach Ibrahim I would be here for the year, if not indefinitely. But my parents hired tutors in the afternoons, and they held me hostage. During my junior year, I also made my high school football team, which was all right with my parents, because it was an extracurricular. Between being inundated with education and school football practice, I could only make Fridays with Coach Ibrahim. Despite my desperate efforts to be there, Ibrahim was displeased with my absence. He was frustrated with me because I was one of his best players, and though he was strict on us, I was present enough to stay on the team. But for the majority of junior year, I was a sedentary player: a sub at the end of a game, but essentially a benchwarmer. For that, I resented school all the more.

Senior year, called *tawjihi* in Jordan, arrived. Jordanian kids studied every day for hours on end. Attendance and participation in school were taken seriously but were not as valuable as the grades received on midterms and finals, which were issued by the government. The pressure made the adults nearly as nervous as the children. God forbid they didn't have the security that a glowing report card provided: a degree and an honest profession with handsome pay. Final grades defined the future. The students with the highest grades were lauded; parties were thrown in their honor.

My dad admonished me. "You'll never amount to anything. If your grades stay the same, you're going to fail in life."

DESTINED TO FAIL

I couldn't care less. On my walk through the neighborhood to football practice, I felt the eyes of my peers. Their attention drifted from their textbooks to the window, where they saw a senior shirking his schoolwork. *He's not studying,* they must have whispered. *What's he doing?*

While the other seniors were academic recluses, I said to hell with it. Making practices and games was strenuous. I didn't have a car and couldn't rely on my parents. I wouldn't dream of asking them for rides. The only answer would have been a stinging reprimand. I relied on public transport and took a twenty-minute bus ride to Petra Stadium. When pressed for time, I used my allowance for a taxi. Sometimes, I jogged to the field. I did whatever I had to, and it paid off. I became no longer a benchwarmer but an active player.

"I'm all in," I told my coach. "I'm going to give the Cubs all I've got."

Ibrahim was taken aback. He knew how important senior year was. "Really?"

"Really," I said. "I know I'm not going to get the highest grades, so what's the point in studying?"

I relished the inherent obstacles of football. The hard-jawed, stocky defense saw it as a game of willpower and force. I was an intrepid offensive player. To me, football was instinctive, strategic. Ibrahim saw my potential. I was the goal-scorer and one of his top five players.

"Keep it up," he said. "I hope you're not leaving anytime soon."

"Don't worry," I replied. "I'm not going anywhere."

At the start of senior year, I thought, *I really need another friend*. I sought out the others who had silenced themselves and managed to find one. His name was Fadi, and he was quieter than I. We stuck together and looked over, envious, at the other cliques: the popular kids and the troublemakers.

Fadi was like me: he didn't impress his parents with good grades. We were both fresh from other places, I from Khartoum and Fadi from Dubai. We were nobodies who knew no one. The two of us laughed at each other's jokes and stayed friends when no one wanted to associate with us.

On the roof of my house, I raised rare pigeons with unusual markings. They flew over me on their way to somebody on the other side of the city. I caught them in their moments of repose, clipped their wings, and sold them at the pigeon market with my friend.

Early in the morning, we rode thirty minutes on a public bus. We priced our birds high and bought ours low. The pretty males went for five to ten Jordanian dinars. Often, the pigeons we had sold flew back to us, and we'd steal and resell them. It was a small business and a dirty one. This was money I could make myself, especially for taxi and bus rides to football meets. I wouldn't have to ask my prying parents for money.

After dinner one night, I went downstairs to my room, which had a separate entrance. I had been studying for a few hours when there was a tap on my window. My friend who lived across the street waved. I opened the door.

"What's up?"

"Me and the boys are gonna play cards and smoke some hookah," my friend whispered. "Wanna join?"

I peered over my shoulder and looked back at my friend with a shrug. "Sure." I softly shut the door and crept into the night.

I sat in a smoky room with a couple of guys. During the rounds of card games, I took a few hits of hookah. I was cautious; I didn't want it to affect football. *I should get back before my parents find out,* I thought.

An hour and a half later, my neighborhood was dark, save for one room in each house with a light continuously ablaze. A senior sat there, too buried in his books to notice my stealthy walk home. When I padded around to the back entrance, my stomach dropped.

My dad stood by the door. He was angry.

"Why aren't you studying?" he demanded. "Where were you?"

"Playing cards," I said.

"Don't insult my intelligence," he said, sharply. "I smell hookah on you."

"I needed a break from studying."

"Get out."

"What?"

"Get out of this house."

"I can't, Dad. I have to study—"

"*Get out!*" my dad roared. "You're lazy and reckless, and I'm sick of it. Get out of my house!"

I sprinted to where my friend lived a few doors down.

"My dad kicked me out," I said. "Can I call someone?"

I called my aunt's house. Razi's sister, Reem, answered, and I asked if I could stay over.

"I'll pick you up," she said. She drove me to my aunt's, where I spent the night. My aunt called my dad.

"What are you doing, throwing him out in the middle of the night?" she asked. "He's got midterms coming up."

The next day, my dad reluctantly took me back in.

"You go back to your room, and you *study*."

At the last Cubs game, my team won 3-0. I scored one goal, and my teammates scored the rest. Afterward, I felt a grip on my upper arm. Ibrahim pulled me aside.

"As soon as the school year is over," my coach said with meaningful intensity, "come see me. You have what it takes. I want a goal scorer, and you're definitely on your way. With some training and working out to put some muscle on you, you'll be ready. I have no doubt that, in a couple years, you'll be a starter for the top team."

"Yes, sir," I said.

DESTINED TO FAIL

I walked to the bus stop, past vendors overflowing with merchandise, brown compact storefronts, and men with tired faces on their cigarette breaks. Cars and trucks sang along the busy street. *I'm sixteen, and I just got recruited for pro football.* I couldn't believe it. I gaped at myself in wonder.

On the bus, I replayed Ibrahim's words. "You have what it takes." I couldn't stop smiling. The rest of my life awaited, perilous and thrilling. My future was secure. I knew I'd be all right.

A month before exams, the seniors retreated to their rooms and shut the door. They weren't seen at school, not to mention in the outside world. For thirty days, they starved themselves of sleep and memorized grammar and equations. June 13 was my seventeenth birthday, and Fadi and I spent it in the exam room. For two weeks, the exams were given every other day. I circled answers with the knowledge that the results would disappoint my parents. Of course, I wanted to pass, but with just enough to escape.

I had found my calling. Life had led me here. During my childhood, I had been in continuous motion from one place to another. I had seen drastically different cities and made and lost friends in an instant. In football, I'd run far, but the bodies beside me had remained steadfast. This was an unconventional form of work, but it was something I loved. I bubbled over with excitement to tell Ibrahim I was ready.

In late June 1993, once I had finished my last exam, the confines of a desk and chair were behind me. I was high on liberation and wanted to sit on the curb with my friends and tell Razi about my recruitment.

When I walked into the house, a familiar whiff of lemony warmth met me from the kitchen. My parents were setting the table for dinner.

"How did you do on the exam?" my mom asked.

"I'm done," I said. I plopped myself down at the table. "That's all I care about. I don't want anyone to bother me with anything this summer. I'm going to play football full time."

"We need to talk," said my dad.

Fantastic, I thought. *Another talk about my future. Yes, my grades are bad, and I won't go to med school. But I'll show them, I'm going to make it.*

My mom served dinner and sat down. She was solemn.

"High school is over now," my dad said. "I have plans for you."

I spooned some food onto my plate. "What kind of plans?" I asked, unenthused.

"Just like your older brother went to America, you will, as well. We're going to your sister's. Afterward, you'll go live with your uncle, and attend the university where he teaches, so he can watch over you."

"Unless my uncle lives in Amman," I said, with my mouth full, "I'm not going anywhere."

"I already bought you a plane ticket."

DESTINED TO FAIL

"Well, we'll worry about that in August. I'm going to play football for Coach Ibrahim this summer."

"That's not going to happen."

Something had shifted in the house. A dark spell had settled on my parents, who knew something I didn't.

"Why not?" I asked. "I worked hard this school year. I should have a summer for myself in Amman, don't you think?"

"You won't be staying in Amman this summer," my dad continued. "You are leaving for America tomorrow morning."

"*Tomorrow?*" I shook my head. "I'm not going to America. I don't want to leave Jordan."

"It's what's best for you," my dad said.

"*I* know what's best for me, and it's not leaving Jordan."

"The flight leaves tomorrow morning. You and I are going to America."

I looked at my mother. "Mom, is this true?"

"It's what's best for you," she said, her eyes downcast. "You'll go to dental technician school. You'll start your life there. You'll be safe with your uncle, and it will be better than here."

I was incredulous. "Dental technician school? I don't know how to speak English!" *This can't be happening,* I thought. "Why can't I stay in Amman for the summer, at least until August? Give me a chance to make the team."

"We're leaving in the morning, and that's final," said my dad. "Go pack your bags."

"Mom, why aren't you going?" I asked, unable to hide my desperation.

"I can't go. I have to stay here," she said, softly. "Your father is the one who will take you and then come back."

"I don't want to go." I pleaded, "Tomorrow is too soon. I won't be able to say goodbye to my friends or anything."

"You have no choice now," my dad said. "All the plans are final."

The look on his face told me what I needed to know. I couldn't argue.

Later, I called Razi. "I'm leaving for America tomorrow," I said slowly, still trying to comprehend it. The words on my tongue felt odd. I didn't believe myself. "My dad's taking me. I'm going to dental technician school."

"Yeah," Razi said, sounding glum. "I heard. My parents know, and we're coming over to your house later."

"I still can't believe it," I said.

Packing my suitcase felt strange. *Should I go to Coach Ibrahim?* I wondered. *Maybe I should apologize.* I couldn't find it in myself to face him. My coach, my friends, my commitments had been dashed to bits. My dad had torn it out of my hands; he'd deemed it all unworthy.

Razi and his parents came by the house. I hugged my cousin, unsure of when I'd see him again. The following morning, I stuffed my bag in the trunk of the car. Fadi,

DESTINED TO FAIL

Amjad, and my other friends would wake up, blissful and oblivious to my departure. I pictured Ibrahim sitting eagerly by the phone with his morning tea. The image stung my eyes as the car rolled down the street.

The ride to the airport was silent. For the last time, I visited the familiar in my mind. The City of Petra, which I'd explored with my friends and where ghosts had whispered to us from the sandstone cliffs. The stadium where I'd made the professional team. I watched the street rush by, and it felt final. I didn't know when I would see this place again.

My mom was undone at the airport. I knew none of this was her idea. She held my hand as we walked to the gate, and she wept into my shirt as we hugged. I cried. Her arms gradually loosened.

"I don't want to leave Jordan," I said through tears.

"It's what's best for you."

I followed my unfazed father through the airport. I turned around and gave my mom a last wave.

On the plane, the smiling flight attendants told us to fasten our seatbelts. I cried as the pilot spoke soothingly over the intercom. I held Jordan, the land and its bighearted people, in my sights for as long as I could. *I might not see this place again.*

ANAS AFANA & STELLA BELLOW

THE CORNFIELDS

On the flight from Amman to Amsterdam, I didn't look at my dad. *I don't speak the language of where I'm going.* The thought trapped me in my seat. My anxiety grew feverish and turned to rage. *Football was my dream. Dad robbed me of it.* I wanted to punch something; the back of the seat in front of me looked good enough. Yet, the next minute, the anger vanished. I thought of my mom and cried.

The layover in Amsterdam was nine hours. My dad wanted to tour the city. We caught a bus from the airport and walked downtown, where the locals openly smoked weed on the street in the light of day. I thought that was outrageous. We ate lunch and poked around a souvenir shop. I couldn't enjoy any of it, though. I was in disbelief. *What the hell am I doing in Amsterdam right now?*

My dad and I passed a storefront where sleek high-tops and basketball shoes were on display. I had worn a pair of dress shoes for the plane, and my feet were sore.

17 in Amsterdam, wearing my new shoes

My dad saw me eyeing a pair of sneakers with *CONS* in stylish block letters on the front.

"You want those?" he asked. "You need an upgrade." In his own way, he was trying to cheer me up.

"Yeah," I said, ambivalent. *I don't want stuff, I thought. I just wanna go home.*

"Let me get you a pair."

They were slick, and my feet were finally comfortable. My dad, well-traveled and street-smart, took us on the train to different parts of the city. He took pictures of me as we walked around.

"Come on," he said, irritably. "Smile."

I didn't offer smiles. I was bitter. When the time came, we rode the bus back to the airport. My exhaustion was so profound, it subdued my grief. I already missed my mom.

When the plane took off from Amsterdam, I spoke quietly to my dad.

"Where exactly does Suhair live?"

"A town called Iowa City," he answered.

"Where's that?"

"The closest major city is Chicago."

We flew from Amsterdam to Minneapolis. There, we boarded a small plane to Cedar Rapids, Iowa. When we descended, I thought we were landing in an ocean. Tea-colored water submerged the houses, the roads, and the trees.

DESTINED TO FAIL

The air was muggy when we got outside. My sister's husband picked us up in a gold Oldsmobile. He explained that the interstate was closed because of the massive flooding. We would have to detour, and the normal thirty-minute drive from Cedar Rapids to Iowa City would take an hour and a half. It was a historic flood, my brother-in-law explained. People were dying and without running water. U.S. President Clinton had declared the entire state of Iowa a federal disaster.

We arrived, bleary-eyed, to Suhair's place on the outskirts of Iowa City. She and her husband lived in an apartment complex. Her joy at seeing me was nearly drowned out by an infant's cry from the other room.

That night, I couldn't sleep. The upset of the last twenty-five hours made me restless. Still on Jordan time, my eyes were wide at 5:00 in the morning. Abandoning my attempts to drift off again, I put on my shoes and crept through the sleeping house, down the hall, past welcome doormats, and down two flights of stairs. I stepped outside and quietly shut the white metal door behind me.

I had no concrete concept of where I was. The morning was still dark, save for a pale wisp of light gaining strength overhead. I stood on a roundabout lined by long, brick apartment complexes. The circular road jutted into parking lots and looped into a small neighborhood.

I walked down the lane shaded by black locust and hickory trees, and I stopped where it diverged onto a main road. To the right would lead me to the city; to the left, the country. But I didn't know that yet. I turned left.

I came to a highway. A few cars hurtled by. I walked in a ditch between the road and a field as the sky grew lighter. For a few miles, I kept on in this direction. *Maybe if I keep walking, I'll see buildings. A city or something.* I waited to see skyscrapers emerge from the distance. Yet nothing but stalk after stalk of the thick reeds that grew beside me.

Holding my nephew, Jawad, next to the gold Oldsmobile, 1993

A breeze from the oncoming traffic funneled through the cornfield. My eyes landed on something lying ahead, a long, leafy vegetable. I picked up the ear of corn and inspected it. Slowly, I took it apart from the top. In Jordan, I knew about corn, but I had never seen the stalk, with its roots in the earth and an upright tuft of flaxen hair. *So, this is where corn comes from*, I thought.

As I walked back to my sister's house, the sun's rays grew warmer. The highway hummed with commuters. The house was awake when I arrived.

"Where were you?" asked Suhair.

"I found corn!" I said. "There's *so* much corn."

"We're in *Iowa*," she said with a laugh.

I knew Philadelphia because of Rocky Balboa. Of course, I knew New York City, Los Angeles, Chicago.

But *Iowa*? The word mystified me.

My brother-in-law went to work that morning. The new grandchild transfixed my dad and occupied my sister. I was restless and bored. There wasn't a football in sight.

"*Please,* give me something to do," I implored my sister.

"We have a membership at the field house here," she said.

"What's a field house?"

"It's a sports complex. There's a track, a pool, a basketball court. You should go."

I rode my brother-in-law's bike a little ways into Iowa City, to the field house. The disquiet in my mind subsided as I tired myself out in the swimming pool and jogged a few laps on the track. Adrenaline expelled the sick, stagnant feeling I'd gotten from airplanes and cars, and I was myself again, until I entered the men's locker room.

Men there laughed and talked gregariously as they flung their swimsuits to the ground, revealing hairy behinds. My ears went red, and I felt faint. Everything was everywhere.

I rushed back to my sister's.

"Everyone in the locker room walks around naked!" I whispered in horror. In the Middle East, I had barely seen an inner thigh.

"Oh yeah." Suhair laughed. "They do that here in America."

I was not inside the spectacle of an American city that beckoned from the television. I wasn't in a galaxy of dark, glass high-rises and ornamented buildings. Instead, I found myself in a silent box. A country of rolling flatlands, highways, and agriculture. A land that waited for a swollen river to decimate it.

The plan was, in two weeks, to drive east. My uncle, the professor, taught at Indiana University of Pennsylvania. I had met my uncle once before. He was the opposite of my father, a gentle, affectionate man who taught finance and banking.

In the weeks before we left, my dad and I stayed with my sister and her family. My sister cooked; I ate. I mindlessly flipped through channels on the TV. There were no Arabic subtitles, so I watched in absent-minded boredom, listening to the laugh tracks.

DESTINED TO FAIL

One morning during our second week in Iowa, my dad mapped our route to Pennsylvania. Then, my brother-in-law drove us for twelve hours, as flat monotony and eighteen-wheelers sped past. The expansive sky dwarfed the Oldsmobile as it hummed along the expressway.

"How long are we staying at my uncle's?" I asked.

"I'm not staying," my dad said. "Once I get you set up there, I'm going back to Iowa City."

"What about me?"

"You'll stay with your uncle and go to college there. It'll be like when your brother came here for his engineering degree. He'll watch over you while you go to dental technician school."

"So, you're dropping me off and heading back to Iowa City. Then what?"

"I'm flying back to Jordan," said my dad.

"I want to go back to Jordan with you," I said.

"That's not an option, I'm afraid. Your future begins here. You'll be in good hands with your uncle. He'll help you and take good care of you."

We drove through the outskirts of a city and rounded the bottom of a Great Lake. As the car hurtled through the Midwest, we passed small towns with neat houses and potted flowers.

I felt a pang as I remembered Ibrahim and our unresolved agreement. *Maybe I could play football here*, I thought. Yet Iowa had been devoid of it. People here didn't seem to like football. I had seen America's athletic dominance during the Olympics. I knew about American football and baseball from grainy televisions, shows with beefy men bashing in their skulls and lankier fellows casting a ball into the far reaches of the stadium. But this country did not seem to have any of the sport I loved.

I stared out the window. American flags waved from porches with screen doors.

"After college, can I go back to Jordan?" I asked.

My dad shook his head. "You need to forget about Jordan," he said. "The situation there is only going to get worse. You're better off here."

"But, Dad—"

He cut me off and pointed a finger at me. "No *but*. Jordan is over. Your future is here. There is no going back."

I fell silent and from the backseat watched the telephone poles dance past. I was anxious. *At least I'll know my uncle,* I thought.

In the last hour, we reached Indiana, Pennsylvania, the small town outside of Pittsburg where my uncle lived.

I walked into the main office of the university with my father, uncle, and brother-in-law. The college advisor greeted us. My dad asked her about their dental technician program. Her eyebrows furrowed as she leafed through several stacks of paperwork, then she looked at the four of us with mild concern.

DESTINED TO FAIL

"I'm sorry, we don't have a dental technician program here," she said. "We do have a program of dentistry, but nothing that specific."

My dad was baffled. "Where could we find a dental technician program?"

She replied that dental technicians went to two-year colleges. "There are programs in Texas, California, Iowa, Alabama—"

"Iowa!" my dad interrupted. "Where in Iowa?"

"Kirkwood Community College in Cedar Rapids."

Cedar Rapids was only thirty minutes north of Iowa City. My dad and my brother-in-law looked at each other, dumbfounded.

A weight lifted as the four of us drove to my uncle's house. My fervent prayers seemed answered. *I'll go back to Amman. Dad will forget all about this. I'll call Coach Ibrahim.* I imagined playing for the national team, a septagram on my heart and a red stripe leaping from my white uniform as I raced down the pitch, fans screaming until their voices gave out.

Please let me go back to Jordan, I thought.

I sat with my male relatives in the living room.

"He could stay with his sister in Iowa City," my uncle suggested. He shot me a sympathetic glance. "He could commute. It's only thirty minutes each way."

"That won't work," my dad said. "She lives in a small apartment with a new baby. That'd be tough on everybody."

"Could he stay with his brother?"

"His brother is in the Air Force. He's on base in the middle of nowhere," said my dad. "And I'm sure there's no dental technician school in rural Missouri."

My dad turned to my uncle and threw up his hands. "I have to sign him up in the dental technician program in Cedar Rapids. He has to live on his own."

My brother-in-law always agreed with my dad and nodded his head. My heart dropped to my stomach. "Live on my own?" I cried out. "I don't know any English!"

"You will learn," said my dad.

I'd had enough of everybody. I stood up and went downstairs to see my younger cousins. The drive to Suhair's was quiet. Back in Iowa City, my dad relayed the new plan to Suhair after deciding that the three of us would go see the college in a few days. I agreed to none of it. My hopes dimmed.

In mid-July, we drove thirty minutes north to Kirkwood Community College. I stared out the window. In the cycle of culture shock that had marked my childhood, this was the most jarring. I had experienced contradiction before: the roaring heat of Khartoum contrasted with cold, statuesque Paris. In Iowa, though, reality became ever stranger.

DESTINED TO FAIL

The Kirkwood campus was green and spacious. Summer had emptied it of students. Linn Hall, the main student center, was a brown, mammoth building. I followed my dad and my brother-in-law through its heavy doors in search of the international students' office.

Gayle, the advisor, greeted us. She radiated warmth and maternal sensibility. She went into detail about the great ESL program at Kirkwood. I would need to complete a year of it prior to my courses in the dental technician program. Gayle gave us a tour and pointed to a classroom.

"That's where your ESL classes will be," she said, cheerily. She led us to the dental laboratory. "You'll be in this room in a year."

My dad looked around, impressed. I stood there and nodded. In Jordanian high school, everyone had been fluent in English. I had learned French in Sudan, because that was the second language among the Egyptian teachers. I had studied some English in Jordan, but really, I knew nothing. I watched Gayle's lips and caught one or two words. She talked in a fast string of syllables that my dad was fluent in.

My dad and my brother-in-law spoke on my behalf, and Dad signed me up for community college. He paid for the first semester up front.

Gayle sent the three of us across the street, where my dad could pay for the dorms. My room had beige walls, a mattress, a dresser, and a recliner. We met the manager, and my dad paid for three months of rent.

Back in the car, I didn't speak. I felt kicked in the stomach. I watched the strange world rewind until we were back in Iowa City.

August rolled around, and the idea of home receded further. I threw a small bag in the trunk of the car, and my dad and brother-in-law drove me to Cedar Rapids. We stopped at an Econofoods, a fortress of a supermarket that blasted air conditioning and played happy-go-lucky pop music. We bought a few groceries and then drove to the college.

When we arrived, the dorms were deserted. The parking lot was empty.

Is my dad really going to leave me here?

I had shut the thought out before. This time, though, I begrudgingly faced it. Even at my uncle's, as I'd listened to the conversation, the concept had been unthinkable. Now, it was becoming real.

I took milk, eggs, bread, baloney, a box of cereal, and a few cans of tuna out of the plastic bag and put them in the dormitory fridge. I tossed my overnight bag on the bare mattress. Dad counted some bills from his wallet and handed me a wad. Four hundred and fifty dollars.

I followed my sister's husband and my father into the parking lot. *This isn't really happening.*

"Bye, Anas. Good luck!" said my brother-in-law before getting back in the Oldsmobile.

DESTINED TO FAIL

The sun behind my dad cast a stark shadow on the countenance that made grown men fear him.

"Well." He exhaled. "This is it. You're on your own. If you make it, great. If not, you were destined to fail, anyway."

ANAS AFANA & STELLA BELLOW

PART TWO
SURVIVAL MODE: 1993-2014

ANAS AFANA & STELLA BELLOW

DESTINED TO FAIL

THE NIGHTMARE

The Oldsmobile ambled out of the lot. My father and brother-in-law made the final right turn to meet the highway and soon were an insignificant speck on the busy road. I blinked, and the car was gone.

I stood in front of the dorms in the formidable expanse of the parking lot. Three minutes felt like an hour. I stared out at the road, a world ahead.

They're gonna turn around, I thought.

But there was no sign of the Oldsmobile on the horizon. My grip perspired around the wad of cash in my left palm. The sun was still up, but the Earth felt dark. Terror slid up from the base of my stomach. I wanted to call my mom.

My eyes watered from squinting. I walked back up the stairs to the dorm and stood alone in the kitchen. I didn't feel seventeen anymore. My friend wasn't there to run with me through the alleyways of a strange city. I realized I had never truly been away from my mother. There was no phone in my room, and to think about finding a way to call her was overwhelming. Nomadic loneliness was something

I'd grown accustomed to; it was the domain of ambassadors' sons. This was different: I felt abandoned.

I walked across campus to assuage my isolation and explore my new surroundings. A few people milled about as I wandered through Linn Hall, but they spoke a different language and laughed at jokes I didn't understand. Communication had served me all my life. I could make friends with anybody; if I were stranded in the desert, I'd win over the scorpions. Today, it failed me. Discouraged, I walked back to my dorm.

That night, I lay on my back and stared at the ceiling. Nobody had thought to give me a pillow or a blanket, so a few balled-up T-shirts cushioned my neck, and I covered myself with a light jacket. The backs of my legs were plastered uncomfortably to the hard mattress. I thought the plane ride from Jordan had been the worst moment of my life. But I remembered my friends and my mom and Coach Ibrahim, and they all seeped into a void that would persist in my mind for years.

Silence enveloped me. I listened to my heartbeat. My breath was a solitary sound that told me how alone I was. Exhaustion overcame me eventually, and I fell asleep.

The following day, I tried not to wallow. I made subpar eggs and wolfed them down. Then, I put on my tennis shoes and went for a run. This was a catharsis. Adrenaline rushed in, and fear began to slough off my shoulders.

DESTINED TO FAIL

I took a left on the highway and kept on for half a mile, passing a gas station and a Hardee's. I ran as far as I could into the residential neighborhoods, where American flags waved from well-kept porches, and a pick-up truck sat in every other driveway. Eventually, I reached the edge of Cedar Rapids, then sprinted back to the dorms.

After a shower in the dormitory bathroom, I sat around on the brown recliner and stared out the window. I dug through my luggage and fashioned a baseball-sized football from a couple of socks, then kicked the flimsy polyester-and-cotton thing around until the lock sounded at the door. Holding my ball of socks, I greeted my new roommate in my poor English.

This guy was strange. His name was Brian; he was from Chicago. In our small interaction, I struggled to piece my words together, while Brian gave lazy, one-word responses. The end of the conversation arrived when I asked him a question and he looked away. It was clear. *He's ignoring me because I don't speak English.*

Another noise at the door signaled the next roommate. The new guy walked in with his girlfriend; both smiled and said hello. My new roommate's name was Jeff. He was sandy-haired and warm, and he looked to be a few years older than me. He instantly tried to communicate, seeing we didn't have a language in common.

I relaxed. *At last, some life in this awful place.*

After his girlfriend left, Jeff looked at me.

"Are you hungry?" he asked, putting his hand on his stomach.

I nodded. I was starving.

"Do you like pizza?"

"Pizza," I said, nodding in agreement as I made a triangle with my fingers.

Jeff hooked up the phone for his room and then went behind the door and searched among the coupons. He emerged with the cordless phone and began to dial a number. Jeff said with assurance, "We'd like a delivery." He ordered, gave our address, and hung up.

Twenty minutes later, a red-eyed dude appeared at the door holding a box.

"Five dollars," the delivery man said flatly. Jeff gave him six.

The fresh-baked smell of cured meats and crust made my mouth water. Jeff opened the box. Pepperoni slices sat on a steaming sea of melted cheese. In Jordan, pizza was expensive. I wanted to give in.

"Pork?" I asked Jeff. I knew this word in many languages.

"Nah, dude. It's beef," Jeff said nonchalantly, taking a slice for himself.

I shrugged and ate half the pie.

As we ate, Jeff realized the language barrier was an exciting challenge.

"Girls? You like girls?" he asked.

DESTINED TO FAIL

I understood and nodded vigorously. Jeff's mere presence made me feel worlds better. Eventually, we each went back to our rooms, and I slept, my distress settling a little.

Class started at 8:00 a.m. on the first day. When I arrived at the International Students' Office at 7:30, my insides churned. I scanned the office for someone to make friends with, and my eyes landed on a face that looked vaguely familiar.

This guy is from Jordan.

I walked over to him and asked him, in Arabic, where he was from.

"I'm from Jordan," he said, filling out some paperwork.

Oh, thank God. "Me, too!"

The Jordanian, whose name was Khalid, looked up in amazement. We talked for only a minute, because he was busy.

"But I'll meet you at this spot in the afternoon," he said.

The next guy I met was Lebanese. His name was also Khalid. He introduced me to some other guys from Lebanon and Syria. I liked every one of them, yet the introductions rang with a familiar anxiety. *If they find out I'm seventeen,* I thought, *they won't be friends with me.* Though I had always looked much younger, I had refined how to act older in high school, how to hold myself the way nineteen-year-olds held themselves. My feelings of inferiority and exclusion still lingered.

After the morning classes, I met Jordanian Khalid for lunch and explained my predicament.

He looked at me aghast. "Four hundred and *fifty*?" he said. "That won't last long. Do you have a job?"

"No." I had never held a job in my life. "But I need one."

Khalid made me realize how little money I had. My dad had been skeptical that I would last four months at this school, and he had only paid for one semester, because he thought I was an unreliable investment. To dwell on coming up with money for a second semester was unbearable. I decided not to worry about it until the time came.

"Do you have papers?" Khalid asked. I didn't know what that meant. He explained to me that it was foreigner slang: to work here legally required a permit.

"So, do you have a permit to work here, in the States?" he asked.

"No," I said.

"Then you don't have papers," Khalid said. "But I know a guy. He owns a restaurant, he's Lebanese, and he'll pay you cash."

I ate lunch among the international students. Again, I intuitively recognized a face.

This guy is Sudanese.

I walked over to a black guy waiting at the desk. My Sudanese Arabic was still fresh, so I introduced myself. The guy's jaw dropped.

"How do you know Sudanese?" he said, marveling.

DESTINED TO FAIL

I would never tell anybody there about my dad. A spoiled, carefree version of myself had fled, and a great iron door to my past had clanged shut in my mind. Childhood was dead to me now.

"My dad is in a management position at a company," I lied. "They make him travel to every location to make sure everything is operating properly. One of the locations is in Sudan. I lived there for five and a half years."

"No way!" said the guy, whose name was Ahmed. He called over to four of his friends. "This guy lived in Sudan!"

I told them how the kids called me *halabi* at Sudanese public school, and they got a laugh out of that. They were solemn as I explained my being left to fend for myself in the middle of Iowa. In an attempt to lighten the mood, one of them slapped me on the back.

"Now you get to live the American Dream!"

What's that? I wondered.

"Do you have a job?" Ahmed asked. I told him I was meeting Khalid here, and we were going to drive north to meet the mythical Lebanese man.

Ahmed and his friends nodded knowingly. "Stick with him," they said. "He'll pay you cash. Keep it hush-hush."

Ahmed told me about taxes, permits, paperwork—all the IRS stuff. Also, what "under the table" meant. I tried to absorb it all.

Ahmed gave me his number. "I'll see you here every day, okay?"

The Sudanese kids took me in. I remembered how generous Sudanese people were. Ahmed and his friends were no different.

I went to my afternoon classes and, afterward, met up with Khalid. Khalid and I drove twenty minutes from Cedar Rapids to an Italian restaurant in Marion, a small town fifteen minutes north. When we walked in the side door of the kitchen, the smell of garlic hung in the air. Two chefs were working that day. One stirred a large vat of something, another stood over a pan of spitting oil, and a dishwasher ran plates under a faucet, then set them up to dry.

Khalid asked for Eli.

"He's in his office," one of them said.

As Khalid and I approached the office, the door swung open, and a large, mustached Lebanese man walked out. He saw Khalid and greeted him. In Arabic, Khalid introduced me to Eli, the manager. He was pleased to meet another Jordanian.

"Do you have papers?" Eli asked.

I knew what that meant and said no.

"That's all right. I'll hire you as a dishwasher. Salary is four dollars an hour."

"Thank you! I'll take it," I said.

I agreed to start on a Monday at 4:30, since the last class of the day let out at four. It was only on the ride home with Khalid from the Italian restaurant that a sobering truth dawned on me. I didn't have a car.

DESTINED TO FAIL

I'll walk there, or I'll run, if I have to, I thought as Khalid pulled up to the dorms.

Back in my room, I ordered another pepperoni pizza. It was cheap and the only thing I knew to do. *This beats baloney sandwiches.*

Jeff and I talked as I ate. Jeff had a car, and when I finished my pizza, he drove me to a department store. I bought fitted sheets and blankets. When we arrived back at the dorms, Jeff went back to his room, while I made my bed then turned out the lights.

And all in one day. My head hit the pillow.

LIFELINES

At 7:30 the next morning, I spotted Ahmed back in the International Students Office.

"Hey," he said. "How'd it go?"

"It went really well," I replied. "But I don't know how I'll get to Marion and back. I don't have a car."

"Don't worry about it!" Ahmed said, good-naturedly. "I'll take you."

I weighed the options for my own mode of transportation. Once I discovered Goodwill, I arrived at the idea of a bicycle, which seemed sensible and affordable. I bought a silver street bike for $20, which made my usual eight-minute trip to school take about sixty seconds. I used it for short trips, since work was too far a bike ride. For now, though, I relied on my new friends, who were happy to drive me each way.

My antipathy toward school let up a little on the day I saw a neon-colored flier pinned to the main hall bulletin board. A grainy graphic illustrated a goal and a ball with a hexagonal pattern. I popped around the corner to speak with the woman working at the desk.

"What is this?" I pointed to the flier.

"That's for the soccer club," she replied.

"What's soccer?" I asked.

"You might know it as football," she said.

My eyes got big.

"It's mostly international students on the team," she went on. I grew antsy. "You'll want to talk to Jim. He's a professor of agriculture and the coach. He's in Washington Hall, so you'll have to take your car. It's a five-minute drive."

I left my bag with the lady behind the desk and sprinted across campus. Fueled by a shred of hope, I appeared in front of Jim's office, drenched in sweat. The professor opened the door. He was balding and mousy and wore a button-down shirt with a pen in his breast pocket. A look of mild surprise decorated his face as he studied me there, winded.

"Yes?"

"Are you the coach?" I asked.

"Yes," said Coach Jim. "Do you play?"

I nodded my head vigorously. "I'm *very* good!" I said the same assurance in my voice that Jeff used to order a pizza. I quickly made a mental list: practice for tryouts; ensure I was on par; get back in shape.

"Where are you from?" Coach Jim asked.

"Jordan," I said.

"Oh, we don't get many Jordanians over here. You'd be the first one I've coached." He nodded. "So, you wanna be on the team, kid?"

"Yeah," I said.

"You got it. How should I contact you?"

"Call Gayle," I said. Gayle was so nice, and I didn't have a phone.

Back at the dorms, I ordered my usual. While I devoured a pepperoni pizza and Jeff busied himself in the kitchen, I called my sister on his phone.

"How are things going?" she asked. She knew I loved food and asked how I had been eating.

"Like a king," I replied. "I eat pizza every day."

"I should tell you," she said, "make sure you specify *beef*. Otherwise, they'll put pork on your pizza. Don't eat any sausage, bacon, or pepperoni."

I looked over at Jeff, eyes wide.

"Oh, I've totally been ordering beef." I amended my order the next time.

I walked into the kitchen on the first day at my new job, having never washed a dish in my life. The aroma of garlic greeted me once more, mingled with cured meats. A few massive pots of marinara sat on the stove, and a patina of day-old tomato sauce stuck to the insides and adorned the exterior. Sauce and scraps of food littered every surface: the sink, the stove, and the preparation counters. Buckets of marinara were kept in a large freezer overnight, which, in the morning, would be dumped into the pots and stirred with a giant paddle.

I surveyed the kitchen in disgust. *Four dollars an hour? For all of this?* But I instantly labored over the grimy city of plates. I was the only nighttime dishwasher on staff.

I scrubbed dishes for the whole of the first week. During that time, I found that 5-7:00 p.m. was not my friend. The dinner window made the cooks seem angry. Dishes and half-eaten meatball grinders flew at me from all sides. Weekends were pandemonium.

At work, while my hands were sudsy, I thought about soccer. On the first day of practice, the team was instructed to meet after class in the main hall, at 6:00. I spotted Sudanese Ahmed and waved.

His arms flew up in greeting. "What are you doing here?"

"I grew up in Sudan! What do you think I'm here for?" I exclaimed.

Ahmed laughed. "Good point."

During a break, Ahmed went outside to catch some air. I sat by myself and waited for him. One boy broke away from his group of friends and sat by me.

"Hey," he said. "I'm Carlos."

I introduced myself and asked where he was from.

"I'm from Panama," he said. "How about you?"

Carlos and I hit it off in our broken English. He was a forward, like me. I told him I'd studied the history of the Panama Canal and had always wanted to see it someday. "Yeah," he said. "It's amazing." He had a kind face, round cheeks, and a sunny disposition that burst the fog of my alienation. Something about him was comforting, as though we'd been childhood friends.

On a particularly busy day in the kitchen, I saw that the bread and sandwich station was empty. The cook who regularly manned it had been caught in a surge of impatient customers. I was a visual learner. I had watched the cook's sloppy efficiency, how he layered sauce before meat. I had memorized the menu and knew every ingredient. So, I rushed over to the bread station and began preparing the orders that streamed in ceaselessly from the machine.

"Those are perfect!" Eli marveled. "How did you learn to do that?"

"I just watched," I said. "I know how."

I continued to wash dishes by hand and, when necessary, took on the meatball grinders. When one of the cooks quit, my job involved less soap and water and more fire and carbohydrates. My new friends were happy to drive me. Free food abounded. Lunch was half-off. If a slice of margherita pizza came back to the kitchen looking untouched, I quickly wolfed it down.

As I continued to work, Eli's prejudice became more apparent. The Lebanese man and I became "us," and the

DESTINED TO FAIL

Mexican cooks became "them." I was aware of Eli's racist stinginess.

I also knew he allowed the staff to eat unclaimed takeout orders. Sometimes, I asked the guys in the kitchen what they wanted for dinner, and when a customer called in, I placed two orders. I hung two tickets, one for the customer and the other for the kitchen. When no one came for the phantom order, the Mexican cooks ate without repercussion. I also snuck food out to feed my friends. I knew I was untouchable, and Eli didn't care. He trusted me.

I covered shifts, taking all the hours I could get. My schedule was weeknights from 4:00 till 10:00 p.m. On Saturdays, my shift was from 9 a.m. to 2 p.m. and then an evening shift starting at 4:30.

"I can close for you, if you want," I said to Eli. He trusted me. The restaurant closed at 10:00 on weekdays, 11:00 on weekends. It was my duty to scrub the floors, the counters, and the pots. I then put lids on the buckets of tomato sauce. Plugging my nose, I wiped down the toilet seat. Finally, I locked the door and gave the knob several shakes to be sure. By then, it was 1:00 in the morning, and Ahmed was waiting out front to give me a ride home.

In a strange way, working relaxed me. My head hit the pillow with more enthusiasm. Income, though scant, became steady. After a grueling shift, though, when my eyes ran over a spotless kitchen, I couldn't believe that, for five hours of work, I had only made twenty bucks.

On my free weekends, I hung out with Jeff. We went to the Goodwill or we grocery shopped for the dorm. My restaurant job allowed me to let go of my worries about spending. I'd been afraid to blow the $450 initially, but earning some extra cash eased my anxiety.

Still, I was vulnerable, and Jeff could see it. He gave me everything short of money. We had lengthy conversations in English, which helped more than the ESL classes ever would.

When I fretted over grammar, Jeff eased me. "It's okay," he'd say, and I learned more when I wasn't nervous. Sometimes, he pointed out objects in the world around us and called them by their English names. Once, he picked up a jar of honey.

"What's this?" Jeff asked.

I replied in Arabic. "*Asal.*"

"No, genius… In English," he said with good humor. "This is *honey*. You can call a girl this, too."

Jeff took an equal interest in me. He was a kid from central Iowa who had never been east of Peoria. He asked me about Jordan. We talked for hours, and Jeff listened intently while I recounted stories of home. He introduced me to his friends and took me shopping. He was of small-town stock: sweet, generous, and grounded. But he was also cool and wore Polos and shorts. Jeff's example helped me assimilate.

DESTINED TO FAIL

I loved my reliable friends, who dropped me off and picked me up from work, but I soon needed my own mode of transportation. I didn't have a driver's license or permit.

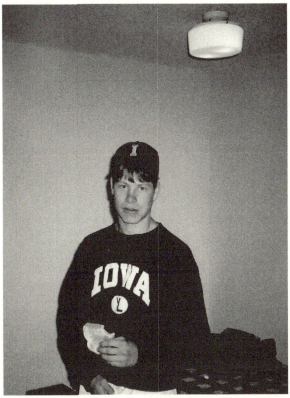
Jeff at college

Jeff wanted to help me get a license, so I could buy a car. He had taken Driver's Ed class at age sixteen, but I had learned through bribery at ten. Jeff took me to the DMV. My sole form of identification was a passport, and I was under eighteen and had never taken Driver's Ed. The only thing I could apply for was a permit.

That night, Jeff helped me study from the book. The next day I took the written test for the permit. I failed once but went back and passed the following day.

When it came time for my driving test, Jeff and I walked into the DMV.

"He can use my car," Jeff said. The lady sat shotgun, staring blissfully at the fall foliage, as I drove Jeff's car around. When we circled back to the DMV, I received my permit on the condition an adult would supervise me in the front seat.

"I'll ride with him," Jeff assured the DMV employees. He was the only person who knew I was seventeen.

I got my driver's license as soon as I could and began saving for a car, the first big thing I'd ever buy. The restaurant job slowly gave me more hours but little pay. As I volunteered for more shifts, twenty hours a week inched into thirty.

Once I had a substantial amount saved, Ahmed took me to a used car lot. A beige '82 VW Rabbit caught my eye. Two of its triangular side windows were missing, and a sign in the windshield flashed a slanted *$899*. I approached the dealer.

"Would you take less for that?" I asked. The dealer declined my request to slice off three hundred dollars.

"Could I give you one hundred to hold it till I come back?" I offered.

"No, sorry," said the dealer.

A few weeks later, when I returned with six hundred dollars in cash, the car still sat in the lot by itself.

"Will you sell it to me now for six hundred?"

"I'll sell it to you for seven hundred," the dealer answered, still insisting on more than I had.

"It's been sitting here for a long time though," I countered. "And it's missing two windows. If somebody wanted it, they'd have bought it by now. I'm not paying more than six hundred."

Finally, the dealer gave in.

When I drove the little Volkswagen I'd bought, the autumn winds whistled through its missing windows. I remedied this with some plastic bags that rattled in the breeze. I told people it was temporary.

I didn't hear from my family much. It was the early nineties, and calls to Jordan cost three dollars a minute. Sometimes, my mom caught me on Saturday mornings at 8:00, before I went to work. That way, I wouldn't have to pay astronomical amounts to call her.

"How are you eating?" she'd ask.

I had occasional conversations with my dad, too. He'd ask about my classes. In the midst of school and strenuous days in the kitchen, I found it easy to fool myself out of homesickness.

Denial consumed me. That I was there and my dad had left me; that I was all alone and had to fend for myself. I imagined buying a ticket home. *How do I even buy plane tickets?* I wondered. In a foreign country, I didn't know how. *How much money would I need? What would Dad say if he found me at home?* In the oppressive dorm, with its beige walls and brown carpet, I dreamt up escapes.

Reality made me sink further into feelings of disappointment. After the first football practice, Carlos and I realized what a joke the Kirkwood Soccer Club was. It did not intentionally deceive: it *was* a club, just not a team. There were no tryouts. The first practice was a casual scrimmage, where it was evident Coach Jim was not qualified. He didn't know offense from defense.

We found out that, long ago, he had been a goalie in an African country, and the coach had assigned him the post because he had no skill on the field. Most of the Kirkwood players were Spanish, and they'd call ¡pasame! to one another. It was too fast-paced for those of us who spoke Arabic; we couldn't catch on in time. Coach Jim was monolingual, and his lack of effort to communicate with anyone made the team suffer.

Kirkwood Soccer Club that year was no better than a punching bag. We served as a warmup for good teams like University of Northern Iowa, Cedar Falls, Maharishi, and Grinnell. Midseason, Kirkwood found themselves up

DESTINED TO FAIL

against Maharishi University, whose players were mostly Brazilian.

Approaching the field, I stared in awe at the opposition. Steam seemed to emit from their nostrils. Maharishi scored and scored, crushing our spirits with their glorious quads. 14-0. Devastating.

If the circumstances of college life didn't bring Carlos and me together by coincidence, one of us made sure to see the other. On Saturday nights, after I got off of work, we drove down First Avenue. I bought an Ace of Base cassette for $5.99, and the speakers shook on the brink of blow-out with nineties pop as we rolled down the street to the Dairy Queen.

The scene swarmed with boys who smiled and wiggled their eyebrows at the girls in the next car over. Here, new friends were plentiful. Carlos and I were out till almost sunrise, music blaring.

When I couldn't cover a shift at work, I went to a party with my soccer friends. There was always one in somebody's dorm after a game, whether Kirkwood won or lost. We were a niche sensation on campus and had an entire fanbase of Spanish-speaking soccer groupies. But the soccer club was weak. Losses were frequent that season.

Soccer came to a close, and winter neared. The ground began to freeze over. In Amman, it might snow. But Jordanian winters didn't venture below twenty-five degrees

Fahrenheit. In Iowa, the winter of 1993 dove into temperatures well below zero, and all I had was a flimsy jacket.

When the bleakest day of the year arrived, I held my jaw to keep my teeth from chattering in the polar temperatures. My car wouldn't start. Like the refrain of a horror movie, I thought I'd perish from hypothermia in the front seat.

I dashed inside, put on all my long-sleeve shirts and a summer jacket, grabbed my things, and ran across campus. The world ahead was completely white. Linn Hall was dark.

A figure materialized in the front office and asked, "What are you doing here? School's canceled." I furiously ran back to my dorm against the wind. Once I got inside, I kicked off my shoes in frustration. Ahmed would have to drive me to work that night.

I learned quickly that the cold froze my car battery. Jeff helped me jumpstart it the next morning. He had shown me the Goodwill, and I immediately went there and bought a puffy winter coat. I had to learn about winter clothes the hard way.

For my first six months in the United States, it was all I could do not to think of Jordan. When I wasn't distracted, the void overcame me. Downtime was the enemy. On Sundays, I didn't work. Jeff sat on his bed, under the Blind Melon poster he'd hung on the wall, and studied or finished the paper he had procrastinated on all week. In the room

DESTINED TO FAIL

next door, with its sad, dark furniture and no posters, I was depressed.

While I fancied myself an adult at seventeen, I never expected to suddenly find myself alone with no family or support. Sometimes, the memory of the wad of bills stuck to my palm brought tears to my eyes. As Christmas neared, I felt my grief become a kind of apathy. My feelings of upset and disorientation were still present, though I stuffed them down to make room for everything I had to do. When I thought of my dad, the resentment I felt toward him still burned hot.

At the end of the first semester, I had a conversation with my dad over the phone. He asked me if I'd passed the first semester of ESL. I told him I had.

"Have Gayle send me a letter," he said, "with a confirmation that you passed."

Gayle followed through and sent him the letter. With this confirmation of my academic success, my dad paid for the second semester. This relieved me. A little.

Jeff and Brian went home to their families for the holidays. Everyone left, and the dorms were lifeless and quiet. I missed Jeff. I had been inseparable from Carlos but couldn't see him, because he stayed with a strict host family. Needless to say, I was not invited home.

Solstice descended, and campus became dark and barren. The phone never rang. During the holidays I spent alone, I lay on the brown recliner, subsumed with memories of Jordan.

Until work began after the holiday weekend, I was miserable, enveloped in the dorm's silence. A relentless wind came down from Manitoba and whistled past the windows.

DESTINED TO FAIL

ILLEGAL SURVIVAL

One afternoon during my second semester, I sat with some guys at lunch in the main hall. They were friends of friends. One guy named Sid ate a sandwich, his brows furrowed, as he listened to his friend, Mo, worry about car payments. Mo had walked into a dealership and made a colossal purchase he now deeply regretted. He'd bought a brand-new Nissan, and his anxiety had worsened as the bills piled up.

"Why don't you sell it?" Sid asked.

Mo dismissed that idea, saying he could never sell the car for what he owed.

"You could, you know, have a 'car accident.'" Sid winked as he put down his sandwich. "Like, you could total it. The insurance company would cover it, and you could pay your car off. Just like that, no more payments."

"How would I do that?" asked Mo.

"Roll it into a ditch or a pole or something."

Mo laughed. "You watch too many movies. I can't do that. That would be *crazy*."

"I could do it," I said, only half-joking.

Mo chuckled. "Really?"

"Sure. I'll drive it into a pole for you." When the group laughed, I ran with the joke. "How much will you pay me?"

Mo smiled. "How about three hundred?"

I shook my head. "Too cheap. I'll do it for six hundred."

"How about five hundred then?" he said. "If you're really serious."

I nodded. "I'll do it for five hundred. But I want the money before. Otherwise, no deal."

"Deal," said Mo.

I looked him in the eye and stuck out my palm. "Shake on it?"

The joke became a reality, and now I was afraid. This was nothing like anything I'd done in Sudan. Wrecking cars for insurance money wasn't funny. This was an adult's crime. But no one was there to tell me no, and it would be a hundred hours in the kitchen to equal this offer. It was my young-person's courage, the absence of logical fear, that made me do it. The only thing I did to pacify the voice of good sense was go to the Goodwill and buy a couple of couch cushions.

Mo and I arranged a time and place where traffic would be scant. I asked my friend Sami to act as a getaway driver. He refused at first, but I assured him he would hardly be involved.

"What do you care if I'm the getaway driver anyway?" Sami asked.

"I'll give you a hundred bucks." I could afford to give him a cut of the five hundred.

Sami's eyes lit up. "I'm in."

I promised him we would flee the scene immediately. I wanted as little involvement as possible, and Mo was responsible for the cops. The light faded as I drove the Nissan to the edge of town. Sami tailed me in his own car. I spotted a telephone pole and made it my target. As I braked, I looked over at Mo in the passenger's seat.

"So, now's the time where you give me my five hundred dollars," I said.

Mo let out a sigh and gave up the cash.

"Now, get out of the car and wait for me here," I ordered, pointing to a safe spot. "Once I crash it, I'm getting out, and you take the driver's seat. Got it?"

Those days, some cars had airbags, but the Nissan didn't. Equipped with the hefty sofa cushions, I spun the car around the block. I revved it to forty-five miles per hour, a sensible speed yet substantial enough. I braced for impact, the cushions in front of me, and tucked my head into my chest. Mo looked on from a safe distance away.

I hurtled toward the designated pole, shutting my eyes as the metal vehicle made a fearsome sound of impact against the rigid object. The hood of the car was in ruins. My collarbone was sore from the seatbelt, but I'd lived. The sofa cushions proved effective.

I breathed in the good air. The adrenaline made my heart pound. I climbed out of the car. As Mo and I quickly traded places, Sami pulled up in the getaway vehicle. I threw the cushions in the backseat, jumped in next to him, and we took off. When we arrived back in the dormitory parking lot, Sami got a hundred bucks for services rendered. He was still wary.

"So, what's gonna happen now?"

"It's not my concern anymore," I said. "I did my part. I got my money. The rest is on Mo to deal with."

"But what if he gets caught and says you did it?" Sami asked.

I smirked. "You and I were playing soccer that whole time, right?"

"Oh." He nodded, smiling wryly. "Yes, we were."

I crawled into bed that night with a freshly washed head of hair and a sore collarbone. I had done something illegal. Guilt and nerves crawled around in my gut. I closed my eyes and vowed to wall it off. This was good money for something done quick and dirty. *And I need it,* I thought. *I got my end of the bargain, and Mo will get his.*

Gayle had called me to the office one day during my first semester.

"We're getting a few international students together to take a picture to promote Kirkwood," she'd said. "Would you be interested?"

"Okay." I'd shrugged, sort of confused, but I stood next to Ahmed and smiled for a photo, tucked in the back because I was tall. Carlos sat in front of us on a stool. Public relations at Kirkwood printed out thousands of brochures with my beaming face among the group of foreign kids. Gayle hung a giant poster of it on her office wall, and then I forgot all about it.

A few months later, in the spring of '94, some international kids came up to me and said, "Gayle wants to see you."

I walked into her office. "Were you looking for me?" I asked.

"Yes," she said. "Someone here is looking for you."

"Who?"

Gayle surveyed the office and furrowed her brow. "I'm not sure. Hang on." She stood up and walked in the other direction. "Hey, where's the new kid?"

I stood and waited. There was a noise behind me, and I turned. It was a boy I knew from somewhere. My wheels turned to recall his face. Before it hit me, Osman opened his mouth to speak.

"I'm *so* sorry, man!" he said, his forehead riddled with remorse.

Under the coarse mass of a twenty-year-old's facial hair, I recognized the boy from Khartoum. A ghost from my past stood, corporeal, before me.

"Osman?"

"They made me write your name."

"My ass still hurts from that day," I chuckled.

"I'm really, *really* sorry. It got out that you were leaving school, and those kids wanted to get you whipped before you left."

I attempted to process it. *The kid who wrote my name on the board in Sudan… Is standing in front of me… In Cedar Rapids… Smack-dab in middle-of-nowhere Iowa, United States of America!*

Osman's trajectory from Sudanese public school to Kirkwood Community College had been a coincidence. He'd stayed in Sudan before going to Montreal for university. Osman didn't feel at home in Quebec, so, one day, he'd called his cousin, Ahmed. This was, in fact, the same Sudanese Ahmed with whom I played soccer, the guy who had driven me to my job and explained what taxes were.

"How's Montreal?" Ahmed had asked.

"I hate it here. I'm lonely, and I'm freezing my ass off," Osman had said.

"You should come here, to Cedar Rapids."

"Where's that?"

DESTINED TO FAIL

"Iowa. It's *beautiful*," Ahmed had said. "There are lots of Sudanese guys at my college. And I'm your family."

Osman had transferred to Kirkwood and walked into Gayle's office. He recalled looking at the giant poster of international kids and seeing me.

"Is that guy named Anas?" Osman had asked.

"Yes," said Gayle.

"Is he from Jordan?"

"Yes."

Osman's eyes had grown large in amazement. "I'd like to see him."

I understood why Osman wrote my name on the board. The environment at the Sudanese public school was cruel. Teachers and students alike were complicit in it. They would've beaten him up after school, had he not complied. Osman's appearance still comforted me. *Thank God I know someone here,* I thought. The coincidence boggled and amazed me.

After the serendipitous meeting with Osman, I realized that he was the only other person who knew the truth about my dad's occupation. I worried he might innocently let something slip to Ahmed, and I would come off as dishonest, so I explained to Ahmed what my dad did.

"I didn't tell you because I didn't want you to think I'm some rich kid," I said. "That life is over, and that's how I want it to be. Please don't tell anybody else."

Ahmed understood and reassured me. "It's cool. Your secret's safe with me."

In April 1994, on a slow night working in the kitchen, I was chatting with one of the delivery guys.

"I do roofing during the day," he said. "And my boss is looking for a couple of guys."

"What's roofing?" I asked.

"You see the rubber stuff on top of that house?" he said, pointing across the street. "That's what we do. We rip it off and replace it. Your job would be clearing out everything we tear down."

The roofing job was not under the table, like the restaurant. It factored in taxes and was fourteen dollars an hour. I didn't have papers to work in the States, but I needed the job. Other than a little money from my dad, the restaurant was my sole source of income. What I made covered everyday bills, car repairs, and some spending money.

Filling out the paperwork proved useless. *Not valid for employment* was typed in grim, decisive letters at the top of my Social Security Card. I needed some form of stable, legal work, and I didn't know whether my dad would pay for the next semester. I was foreign, too, which hiked up the tuition to three times the normal rate. The stress of it made the gears of my mind spin.

I went through a mental list of the friends I trusted. I sprouted a brave idea, and told Khalid about my need for the job.

"Could you make me a copy of your Social Security Card?" I asked.

Khalid was flabbergasted. "No," he scoffed. "That's illegal."

"Your name won't be on it, I swear. I just need the top part."

Khalid looked at me with a mixture of worry and pity.

"Okay. But I'm still gonna watch you do it."

In the dark silence of the school library after hours, a single scanner whirred. I felt Khalid watch my every gesture as I made a photocopy of his Social Security Card. Then, I made a copy of my own. I slid the scissor blade across Khalid's photocopy and pasted *valid for employment* across mine, then made a copy of that. Once he saw his name was nowhere it shouldn't have been, Khalid approved. The photocopy looked as good as government-issued. I brought the forged Social Security Card to the contractor.

"I lost the original," I told him. "But I have a copy."

The contractor didn't question it.

Jeff was only due to stay for two semesters at Kirkwood. When all his requirements were met, he packed up his room and moved out. I looked into the empty room, at the bare walls, and ached. Jeff had cushioned the blow of my arrival.

He'd helped me with everything, most of all to overcome the initial shock. Things felt rockier without him.

The world was quite inhospitable. I was a vulnerable explorer in the Iowan jungle, focused only on the elements within a six-foot radius. I was cautious, my senses heightened. My ears were sensitive to the rustle of a leaf, the crack of a branch beneath me.

There were people whom I felt comfortable asking for help, and they lent me a hand. While grateful, I was still a scared seventeen-year-old in a foreign country with no papers. In survival mode, I had no choice. Everything made me wary. Even my best friends at school only knew so much. I didn't trust anyone. The only time I felt safe from primal threat was when the door to my room was shut. Even there, I was frightened of solitude.

One day in May, when I had just finished a meeting with Gayle, one of my ESL instructors came into the office. She smiled at me as she stirred her coffee in a Styrofoam cup. I was her favorite student.

She and Gayle struck up a conversation. She expressed, in agony, how overgrown her yard had become.

"You think you could find me a kid to mow my lawn?" she asked. "I'll pay cash."

Gayle cocked her head at me.

"Since it's cash, I bet Anas could do it," she said. "He doesn't have a job. He could use the money."

DESTINED TO FAIL

Gayle knew all her international students' work and visa statuses, so she only knew about my cash predicament. She didn't know I had already booked some jobs.

I looked at the ESL instructor and said, "Sure." *I could always use the money,* I thought. "Where's your house?"

"North Liberty," she said.

My teacher gave me the address and told me the route. When I got there, she had to show me how to use a riding lawnmower. She lived on a farm. There was no grass where I'd come from, but this lady's land rolled from the house to the highway, endless in its supply.

Me and Carlos

In the summer of '94, I awoke in the dark after only four hours of sleep. The roofing job was the most grueling. I had to be at the shop at 5:30 in the morning to load shingles and supplies before we left for the day's work at 6:00. We toiled until 4:00 in the afternoon.

Temperatures on the roof on a hot day shot well above a hundred degrees. I mostly cleared away teardowns, stepping on nails and scraps and shards of things in tennis shoes. It was so physically strenuous that often my back ached and I was lightheaded from the heat. This was five days a week. The yard work in North Liberty was Tuesday and Saturday for two hours. I worked nights at the restaurant. Sunday was my day off.

June 13, 1994 was my eighteenth birthday. Over the last year, loneliness had sucked up my last drop of exuberance. Suddenly, there was no more growing-up to do. One frustration after another had accumulated. I had been driven from my dreams, condemned to survive by the teeth.

Being left in the U.S. no doubt rearranged the chemistry of my brain. Earlier on, my inability to communicate was intensely frustrating. Everything around me was completely new—the systems, the language, and the culture were vastly opposite to mine. The first year was the most difficult. Every interaction in this new language was humiliating.

DESTINED TO FAIL

Me at 18

One day at the restaurant, for example, a lady asked for utensils. I said, "What?" She repeated herself. Puzzled, I went into the back and retrieved a pencil. The lady looked confused and shook her head. "I wanted a fork."

"Oh!" I said, while thinking, *Why didn't she just say* that?

These kinds of things happened all the time, and they made me exasperated. At eighteen, I didn't know how to process or express it. I would erupt unexpectedly, and no one knew the cause. Once, one of my neighbors in the dorms wandered into our kitchen and finished off the last of my milk. I shouted and hurled the empty carton at the wall. The explosions came often and at small things: a perceived slight or a word that rubbed me the wrong way. I needed the anger. Whenever sadness or fear sprang up, I got angry on purpose. It was a release. I blamed my father or anyone else I set my eyes on for this life where I would never play professional soccer again.

I pondered a phrase I'd heard: "the American Dream." The Italians, the Poles, and the Germans had made their fortune here one hundred years before. I thought, *Where's the dream in* this? There was nothing dreamlike about this life, where I was stranded from all I knew.

August 1994 was the end of the year I had paid to live in the dorms, and I didn't understand that my lease needed to be renewed. Dee, the landlady, asked me to have my stuff out by the next day. I asked her why.

"You didn't renew your lease," she said. "I gave your room to someone else."

"Oh," I said, baffled. "I didn't have plans to leave. I didn't know I was supposed to renew anything."

Dee felt bad about it. "Hang on." She riffled through her book and nodded. "I have a room that opens up in four days. I'll give it to the incoming tenant, and then I can give you your same room back," she said. "Don't worry."

I sighed in a mixture of relief and frustration. "Okay," I said. "Thank you."

DESTINED TO FAIL

I felt stupid. All my friends knew what a lease was. My embarrassment was too great to ask for a sofa to crash on. For four days, at a rest stop on Interstate 380 in Cedar Rapids, I slept in my car. There was nothing but clothes in the trunk. Lying in the backseat, I shut my eyes to the hum and exhale of traffic.

When school started up in the last days of August, I began dental technician courses. The year before hadn't felt like college. I had been studying English grammar with other foreign kids and was generally confused. This year was a shift: I worked in a lab and went to lectures and met different kinds of people. I studied with undergraduates and adults alike.

I learned from Gayle one day that my dad had paid for my third semester, my first semester of dental technician school. Amid the work, I was thankful for the help. But this was the last time he helped me with tuition.

He still sent me money whenever he could. It wasn't much, but it helped tremendously with the bills: car insurance, health insurance, whatever was due. At the rate I was working, what my dad sent was minimal compared to what I made every month. I had saved a lot from the summer work, which gave me some more stability and enough pocket money to get by. If I saw a notice for an odd job, I'd take it. My high school self now seemed flighty and far off.

I still worked at the Italian restaurant in the fall of '94. Eli had promised me a raise on the one-year anniversary of my employment. At that point, I practically ran the joint: opened and closed, counted the drawer, dealt out tips, cooked, cleaned, and handled customers. When I asked Eli about the raise, though, he shook his head. He said something about how the restaurant wasn't bringing enough in.

"Are you kidding me?" I said. "We're slammed every night."

Eli was indignant. We argued for half an hour.

"Fine," he finally said. "I'll give you a raise. Four dollars and twenty-five cents an hour. How's that?"

An insult.

"For all I do around here, I want at least seven dollars an hour," I insisted. "If I don't get that, I'll quit."

Eli remained stubborn.

"In that case, you can stick that extra quarter where the sun don't shine," I said and walked to the door.

"If you leave," Eli shouted to my back, "I'll make sure you have problems."

"Well, maybe I'll give Immigration a call," I said. "I'll tell them how you've been treating your employees and how many of them you pay cash." I wouldn't really do that to my coworkers. But that shut Eli up.

A copy of my Social Security Card in hand, I drove to a pizza place that offered delivery. They gave me a job as a driver. Again, I memorized the menu. This restaurant only served pizza; the menu was far easier to remember than Eli's catalog of pastas and calzones and meatball grinders.

On nights when the place got busy, I put on an apron and helped the crew pump out pizzas. The restaurant had two locations in Cedar Rapids, and soon I worked for both.

By March of that year, they offered me the dough boy position. Their guy had quit, and management felt they could entrust me with their secret dough recipe. The position was demanding. It was Saturday and Sunday at 6:00 in the morning. Based on whatever dough numbers were put in by the other restaurant, a certain amount had to be prepared, placed in transport tubs, loaded in the back of the truck, and driven across town. Afterward, the other amount of dough had to be made in-house by 11:00.

Ugh, I thought, *6 a.m.? There goes my weekend.* Then I heard the salary. Thirteen dollars an hour in an air-conditioned kitchen was a good deal. It beat the roofing job from hell, where I neared heat stroke every day for fourteen bucks an hour. I gladly accepted.

Because of work, the dental technician curriculum was often incompatible with my schedule. My shift kept me until the wee hours. In the morning, Betty, the instructor, delivered a lecture about the daily project. This was from 8-9:00, which interfered with my necessary sleeping in. After the lecture, students worked in the lab into the afternoon.

I arrived at 9:30 and whispered to a classmate, "What's the project?" In spite of my spotty attendance, my work reflected attentiveness and care. Betty still noticed my frequent absence from the lectures and disliked me for it.

In class, I befriended two girls my age. Shanna and Melissa were roommates. Shanna was sweet but shy. Melissa was the party girl, the center of attention in any room she entered. I liked the loud ones—they were the girls I hooked up with on the weekends. There was nothing else to do in Iowa but drink and party, and girls like Melissa were a nice distraction.

One night, I dialed Melissa's number. Shanna picked up. "Melissa's not here," she said.

Once Shanna and I started to talk, we connected. My infatuation with the party girl, and all the other party girls, evaporated.

I couldn't be my full self around my guy friends, but I was at ease around Shanna. As we spent more time together, I could tell she cared for me. We spent weekends together and had a favorite spot by the river that we visited over time. Shanna loved bowling, so she taught me how, and many of our dates were at the bowling alley.

She was a great cook, and the first time she cooked us dinner, she made a tater-tot casserole. This was a Midwestern delicacy: ground beef, cream of mushroom soup, green beans, melted cheese, and tater tots. She made me feel at home, which must have satiated some wound from my nomadic childhood. I gravitated toward her.

In the fall of 1994, I called up Suhair. I had visited there a few times since my arrival, since she was my only family close by. "Is it okay if I visit?" I asked. "And can I bring a friend?"

"Of course," said Suhair.

Shanna and I drove down to Iowa City. Suhair cooked us food, and we all ate together. Afterward, Shanna and I, Suhair and my nephew, Jawad, walked to a small playground by her apartment. We spent some time there, then Shanna and I drove back to Cedar Rapids. When I talked to Suhair on the phone later, she said, "I really like her."

A few weeks into December 1994, Shanna invited me to her hometown in northeast Iowa. She was proud of where she came from, and wanted me to see it. Her mother was the town clerk of Postville, Iowa, and her father was a farmer in West Union, Iowa. We spent the weekend driving around in her Ford Escort to visit her divorced parents at their respective homes and narrowly avoided two Christmas dinners.

"Ever driven a tractor before?" her father asked me. He could tell there was no way I had operated a piece of farm equipment in my life.

"No," I said.

"Would you like to drive one?"

Heck yeah, I'll drive your tractor!
"Thank you, sir," I said, containing my glee.

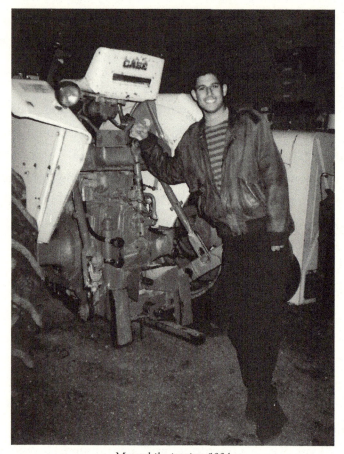

Me and the tractor, 1994

The farm was strange and wonderful. I watched the cows gaze at me with their sweet, unassuming eyes, lazily nibbling the grass. I had gone from seeing an ear of corn for the first time to cows and pigs. Shanna's life in the heartland was surreal to me.

Shanna's father saw the two windows missing on my Volkswagen, and he patched them up with plexiglass. Car rides in the VW were suddenly serene, without the forceful flap of plastic bags.

By this time, in addition to my hectic work schedule, I was the kid who wrecked cars. Word of my operation had spread quickly among the international students. I crashed a Toyota Camry, a truck, and a van, too. Once the damage was done, I would flee. The owner faced the cops, and I had no skin in the situation but the act itself. Five cars met their death by my hand. I was never without a getaway car and an accomplice. Five hundred was my asking price for strangers, due up front. For my friends, they paid whenever they got around to it.

One of my friends relayed the details of an incident that involved an unctuous young man named Hassan. Hassan was part of our friend group of mainly Middle Eastern guys. Hani, my Syrian friend, was dating a girl named Brenda. Hassan cornered Hani's girlfriend while she was drunk at a party, and they hooked up in the backseat of his car. On Hassan's part, it was intentional, since he abstained from liquor. For Brenda, it was a drunken mistake. She came clean to Hani, racked with remorse. He broke up with her.

I watched Hani tremble in powerless anger. "I'm gonna beat the shit out of him," he seethed, and he was almost serious. The friend group banished Hassan after that night, and he wisely kept his distance.

A friend who was still in touch with Hassan called me. "He got hooked on gambling and lost a ton of money," he said. "His dad wants him to move back to Egypt, since he's graduated. But he doesn't want the debt to follow him or for his dad to find out. He wants to total his car, and he wants you to do it. He's desperate, and he wants to leave the U.S. clean."

My loathing for Hassan consumed me. *Now I can avenge Hani.*

I thought carefully. "He's gotta give me five-hundred up front." I drank in my moment of power. "And I want his Super Nintendo. With all the games."

The terms were relayed back to Hassan, and he agreed. I asked around but couldn't find an accomplice soon enough to drive the getaway car. Hassan was liable to change his mind in the next few days or within the week. *And I wanna scare him. He caused my friend pain.*

I knew who to ask. I told my girlfriend the plan and heatedly explained why it was justified. Shanna was convinced and agreed to drive the getaway car.

On the day of, Hassan coughed up the cash and the game console. I gloated over my new Super Nintendo and got in on the driver's side.

"Hassan, you ride shotgun," I said. Nobody ever rode shotgun.

DESTINED TO FAIL

"I was told you'd do this alone and I'd wait by the pole."

"If you don't get your ass in the passenger's seat," I snapped, "there's no deal."

"Okay, okay," he said.

I had my trusty couch pillows along with a rather flimsy one. I was expressionless as I made the preliminary rounds.

"Take this pillow." I gave Hassan the dud. "Buckle your seatbelt."

"Okay."

"Helps if you put your feet on the dash, too."

Hassan seemed to briefly question this then shrugged and did as I said. The bravest speed I could muster was fifty miles per hour. I provided myself with ample cushioning. The car hurtled toward its end. The telephone pole zoomed closer. For a fraction of a second, Hassan's face fell in horror. The car slammed into the pole.

The hood of the car steamed, decimated. My collarbone smarted. I dragged an injured Hassan into the driver's seat. His face was contorted in pain.

"That's for screwing my friend's girlfriend," I said, "you piece of trash."

I slammed the door and sprinted to the getaway car, hopping in next to my girlfriend. Another car pulled up and slowed, its headlights casting a glare on the wreckage. The driver asked what had happened.

"We saw him coming up over the hill," Shanna and I lied. "He must have fallen asleep."

The getaway car was gone before the sirens sounded. Shanna's eyes were wide. For a while, she was silent. Finally, she exhaled.

"That was crazy," she said. "How long have you been doing this?"

"Oh, not long."

I went back to the dorms afterward to see Hani.

"I got even for you," I said and explained the harrowing ordeal.

Hani lit up. He planted a kiss on my cheek. "Thank you."

Shanna sat me down later. "If you keep doing that, you'll either get seriously injured or end up in prison. No more of those."

She's probably right, I thought. I was at peace with five hundred dollars and a Nintendo.

The day after, my shoulder was sore and I couldn't lift my left arm. The cops found Hassan on the driver's side with a concussion and a few minor injuries. We heard about a brief trip to the hospital. Soon, though, he was in better shape. He received his insurance money and flew back to Egypt.

REUNION

Me and Carlos, in cleats

Soccer in the fall of '94 was a riot. Coach Jim was temporarily dismissed by a student named Roger, who walked into rooms with undeniable presence and an air of authority. When he spoke, all fell quiet. Roger played with passion and ruled with discipline. He was unanimously elected team captain.

Jim stepped down in influence: coach might have been his title, but Roger inhabited the position and responsibility.

He held official tryouts, his eye scrutinizing everyone's technique, until twenty were chosen. I found myself on a strong, legitimate team comprised of Latinos, three Arabs (me, Osman, and a Saudi), an American goalie, and a Jamaican named Melvin. A girl named Katie joined us, too. Some of the guys muttered disdainful things to each other about having a girl on the team, but Katie was a talented midfielder, and Roger happily recruited her.

The team members asked Roger why he picked Melvin, who was a gregarious extrovert whom everyone liked, but he was a perennial benchwarmer.

"Every team needs a mascot," he said. "And plus, he's my roommate."

Kirkwood easily won the first match. We won the second, too. We tried not to jinx it as we conquered the following five.

One afternoon, we clambered into the van that took us an hour and a half south to Maharishi University in Fairfield. The ride was quiet: our minds were elsewhere, and our nerves were palpable. When our team arrived, we walked over to the lockers to change. Some staff members at Maharishi stopped us.

"We can't let a team like you use the lockers," they said.

Everyone knew that behavior was partly justified, due to our devastating loss last year. We were still humiliated. Melvin was furious. As we laced our cleats in the van, in his ire, Melvin began to sing "Buffalo Soldier" by Bob Marley.

"'Buffalo Soldier,'" he began, in a voice bold and throaty. "'Dreadlock Rasta....'"

As he sang, our hopes lifted. We joined in, eventually assembling outside the van. A raucous chorus belted the final lyrics as we marched to the field:

"'Woe yoy yo. Woe yoy yoy yo!"

Roger picked his starting eleven. The offensive midfielder from Saudi Arabia, one of the strongest on the team, was missing. He thought he was too good for the van and had driven himself. We looked around nervously. The game began without him.

By halftime last year, Kirkwood was down six goals. This year, it was 0-0. We buzzed with nervous optimism. The Brazilian team members were disoriented, but a potential retaliation was not lost on Roger.

Luis, a defender, took a sharp elbow to the forehead and his eyebrow split open. Coach Jim's wife, Peggy, had appointed herself team nurse and bandaged him up.

Melvin was amped. "Man, we came here undefeated, and we are *leaving* undefeated!" he shouted at us. As Luis heatedly begged Roger to put him back in, the Saudi appeared, forty-five minutes late, in a gleaming-white BMW.

"What?" he said defensively as the team glared. "I got lost."

Roger put a bandaged Luis and the Saudi in for the second half. Fifteen minutes in, a midfielder stole the ball in a counterattack. He passed to me, and my eyes darted around for Carlos. I thought to pass to the left, where my friend barreled up the pitch.

At that moment, someone hollered in Arabic, *"Pass to your right! I'm wide open!"* I was the only person who understood the Saudi, who closed in fast behind me. I tapped the ball to the right. From twenty yards south of the goal, the Saudi intercepted the pass. He kicked the ball, which flew in like a missile, and we scored. Kirkwood lost their minds.

Roger remained vigilant. He subbed out the forwards and played all the defenders, who held it 1-0 for the remainder of the game, and we won. We lost our voices singing and cheering on the ride home.

The party that night raged with cocky athletes and beer. Speakers vibrated with Tupac. The groupies danced and drank.

"I have an announcement!" slurred a flushed Roger, Solo cup in his left hand. He stood on a chair. "Turn off the music!"

Someone stopped the music. Each player's eyes locked on Captain Roger. The room hushed itself.

"This season," said Roger, holding up his arms, "we're going undefeated."

The party erupted.

Kirkwood played their twelfth and last game against Cedar Falls. Our team had maintained an undefeated streak, and at this point, we were cocky. *Why are these guys even here?* we said to one another. *We're gonna beat them anyway.*

The team at Cedar Falls took advantage of our arrogance, scoring two goals within the first ten minutes. When they scored the third, we whipped our heads around in confusion. By halftime, Kirkwood was down four goals. We slunk off the field, our eyes cast on our grass-littered cleats.

Roger pulled his hair out and shouted, "You're all about to blow the *whole* season!"

A few of us stewed in fury; others sank into shame.

Melvin came chin-to-chin with each of us. "Forty-five minutes is all I want!" he shouted. *"Come on!"*

Throughout the next half, Melvin, the hype man, ran up and down the sidelines, yelling words of motivation. When one of our guys was tackled to the grass, Melvin screamed, "Get up! *Get up!*" His voice, incapable of exhaustion, was our fuel.

Roger had supplied us with angry adrenaline. Cedar Falls assumed they would win and grew lazy. Kirkwood whittled down the lead. Melvin leapt up and down. *"Come on!"*

When ten minutes remained, we were one goal away from a tie. Roger crossed the ball to Carlos. From far across the pitch, nearly parallel with the box, Carlos gracefully sprang into the air. He slammed his forehead against the ball, and it hurtled into the goal with two minutes to spare. Kirkwood hollered. We flung our arms around him.

Cedar Falls and Kirkwood tied, 4-4. Melvin didn't play, but we wouldn't have made the comeback without his zeal from the sidelines.

Captain Roger's prophecy came true. Kirkwood went undefeated for the first and only time in the history of the soccer club. We were invited for regionals in Texas, but our unofficial status—a club rather than a team—prevented us from participating. I felt like the main character in a movie. We were the underdogs who had conquered some fearsome soccer warriors.

Besides soccer, I preferred work over parties. On weekends, my twenty-year-old American counterparts were at the bar. They drank with a death wish. Inevitably, a point arrived when someone would tilt precariously forward, fall flat on their face, and stay there.

When I was at an American party and found a friend to speak Arabic with, someone would inevitably turn to us, red-faced, and shout, "Speak English!" At every party, people pressured me to drink. I carried orange juice around in a red Solo cup to curb the ridicule. I avoided that scene, if possible.

When there were no shifts to cover at the restaurant, I partied with the international kids. Instead of rap, people danced to salsa and reggae. The soccer team was there, Melvin and Carlos among them. There, I could relax. People didn't pester me to drink as much. I wasn't nervous to mix up my English grammar. The Colombians and Guatemalans were just getting the hang of the language, like I was.

Melvin DJed these parties. He liked to pull me in close and exclaim: "Jordan. I love Jordan!" Before I could say, "But you've never been to Jordan," he would embrace Carlos. "Panama," he sang. "I love Panama!" I felt out of place everywhere else, yet here I fit in.

As the last weeks of school came to a close, Carlos was among the Latinos who prepared to fly home. I dreaded it. Friends were the best thing here, and they continued to desert me. First Jeff, now Carlos. Shanna and I drove Carlos to the airport. Half my team, kids from Mexico to Colombia, embraced one another farewell. Carlos gave me his aunt's phone number.

I hugged my teammates and held Carlos the tightest. Then, my friend walked to the gate, suitcase trailing behind him. Another one to leave. I felt hollow.

Sometimes, I received an impromptu call from Carlos's aunt's house in Panama. I wasn't so confident in my Spanish, and Carlos was hard to locate on the other line. The ends of the relationship frayed and soon fell to threads.

Coach Jim was happy to see me the following semester at the first practice. Since I was the only returning starter, I had earned the title of team captain. I watched the players run around as awkwardly and clueless as during my first semester. Most of my friends had graduated: Ahmed, Melvin, Osman, Carlos. Another cycle of the Agricultural Program had come and gone.

"You know what, Coach?" I said. "I'm done playing." I walked away.

The autumn ground hardened, and frost crept over the cornfields. In the winter of my senior year, a member of my friend group was killed by a drunk driver. The funeral was a gathering of the devastated. Bitter winds penetrated our black coats. Every mourner wept. I couldn't emote. I questioned why some people were crying. Close friends and the family of the departed I understood, but tears from people who barely knew my friend confused me.

Anyway, he's dead, I thought. *He's better off than I am.*

This thought troubled me. Perhaps it was a symptom of the depression or the lingering shock of my abandonment. My lack of tears and the thought that someone dead was in a better state were revealing. A part of me had withered and died.

Shanna and I got our first place together in spring 1995. We were excited to live off campus and felt like adults in our apartment that cost $360 a month.

We enjoyed living together for the most part, but we got into petty arguments frequently. Shanna liked to say "I love you" a lot. She would say it as she left for work, before we went to sleep, before we ended a phone call—as offhandedly as she said "goodbye."

This was a cultural difference: in Arab culture, we didn't say "I love you" often, and certainly not as casually. I always responded, "Okay, love you," but never felt as though I meant it. *I guess I'm just supposed to say it back,* I thought.

This became the subject of an argument. "Why do you always *say* that?" I'd ask. I thought the phrase was empty and overused. The number of times she said the words seemed to outweigh the times I used them. I didn't understand her expressions of love.

My job was going swimmingly; the restaurant owner liked me. I stood in his office one night as he gushed with praise.

"You're so great with the customers," he said. "You know everything—the dough recipe, the computer system. And boy, do you work hard. The manager at the other store just gave his thirty days' notice. I never imagined giving this job to a nineteen-year-old, but you're really exceptional. We'd like to offer you the position."

"Thank you," I said. "What's the salary?"

My boss told me. It was hefty and included benefits.

"Thank you for the opportunity," I said. "I'll think about it."

I would have been glad to shed the uniform—a black hat and a red-and-white pinstriped T-shirt with the restaurant logo—but the manager's position sounded dull. I liked a job that involved racing around in my little VW. I could compete against the other deliverers and lie about how much I made in tips. All the manager did was sit around, organize papers, and count money. I was on my way to a degree and didn't want to be stuck at a restaurant my whole life.

The assistant manager at my location was named Jackie. She was malevolent and beady-eyed. Everyone hated her. When she got a whiff of my promotion, which she had expected would be offered herself, she grew white-hot with spite.

My deliveries were done at 11:00. I walked into the kitchen with the dirtied pizza trays, loaded them into the dishwasher, and pulled down the lever. I took off my hat, and Jackie immediately insisted I put it back on. I refused. The kitchen was hot; my face got steamed up.

"You'd put it on if it was a head turban I bet," she said with a sneer.

She spat other verbal abuses whenever we were alone. She paired all her insults with *sand* or *camel*. I never reacted, afraid of the repercussions. I was nineteen with forged papers in a foreign country. My feelings of anxiety and loathing went unspoken.

I was under the weather one Saturday night when I was on duty as the designated closer. Determined never to call in sick, I saw the shift through, which always lasted an hour past close, for cleanup. I wanted to go home and lie down. My mood was sour as the deliveries went on.

At 11:05, I brought the delivery trays into the kitchen. *Fifty-five minutes and you're home free.* At that moment, Jackie walked in and announced there was a delivery to be made. She'd taken the call at 10:58. The other drivers had gone home. She knew I was weak and wanted to make my life hell.

I loaded the trays into the dishwasher.

"You're going to have to take it, because I'm not going to," I said.

"You're going to take it whether you like it or not," she countered. "Or I'm going to fire your ass."

She stood behind me as I pulled down the lever on the dishwasher. "Sand n*-" flew from her lips, and the tail end of the slur shocked my system. Jackie leaned on the hard R of the N-word.

I stilled. My hand stayed on the lever. I shut my eyes. "Sand" was geographically obvious. She had used it enough to numb me to it. But the N-word was something heavier. I knew what it meant in America. I realized what she meant in this context: it was in reference to me, to my people.

Mentally, I steadied myself. *If I punch her, I'll go to prison.*

I just wanted to go home. My eyes were on my shoes as I walked past her, intent on the door handle. She followed me. She shouted more slurs as I walked out. I threw the hat at her feet and flung my shirt with the logo on the pavement.

I walked to my car, shivering and half-naked in the March cold. I got in on the driver's side and rustled around in the backseat for a clean T-shirt.

Jackie stood in the doorway, smirking, as I backed out and put the car in gear. She waved, mockingly. I flipped her off and floored it. She returned the bird. *I don't wanna be here.*

The apartment was not five minutes from the pizza place. I drove in loops for fifteen minutes, trying to cool off. I punched the steering wheel then caught myself in the rearview mirror. Something in my reflection upset me. My fist flew up and tore the mirror off its mounting. *I should have punched her instead. That racist bitch.*

I arrived at the apartment complex, my breath keeping time with my angry heart. I tried to compose myself as I walked into the house, where Shanna was watching TV in the living room.

"What's wrong?" she asked, seeing I wasn't myself.

"I quit," I said. "I got into it with Jackie."

Shanna knew about her. "What happened?"

Telling her would only drive my upset deeper. I looked down. "Nothing. She just took a delivery call at 10:58, and I wasn't feeling good. I just wanted to go home."

The owner called the next day. Jackie had complained that I'd walked out on her. She was left to make an entire delivery, mop the floor, clean the trays, and close all by herself. The owner figured something was up. He knew my unrivaled work ethic. I told him everything, including the threat to fire me that was made insignificant by the appalling racial slur.

The owner believed me. "But without proof or a witness," he said, "there's really nothing I can do."

I liked the delivery job, but I asked my boss to transfer me to the other location.

"Whatever it takes to keep you working here," he said.

I quit the location on the southwest end of town, gave up the dough boy position, and moved on to the northeast location. It was the same delivery job, with some occasional work in the kitchen when necessary. I filed the incident deep in my mind, where it would never rise to the surface. There was no one to talk to about it who would be of any help or comfort. I didn't tell a soul.

Vitriolic racism at that level was something I had never experienced. *Halabi* at school in Sudan or "speak English" at American keggers were mere jabs. They were pernicious, yet the offending party had always been more or less my equal. This attack came from an adult in a foreign country. She wielded her power, hellbent on my ruin. I never thought of that assistant manager again, but for a long time, it hurt.

I endured injury on a daily basis. Things I learned the hard way. The conversations in English where I froze, unable to remember a certain word. Racism was the most malignant. While I had good friends and a girlfriend who cared for me, I was like a grenade. My explosions were sparked by everything, and they rose up in my chest and consumed me. I threw chairs and broke objects. On the road, I flipped birds and slammed my foot on the gas, bursting with rancor. There was a time when I'd known myself. I remembered a happy-go-lucky kid to whom things came easy. Here, I was without the safety net of family, of my father, and I didn't really trust anyone. Standing up for myself was a risk. I felt unsafe, alone, with no armor.

In April, my car sprung an odd leak. To fix it at the shop would have required hundreds of dollars I didn't have. I called up my brother, who was a skilled mechanic.

"You think you could make it down here?" he asked.

"I don't know, but I could try."

My brother told me to come visit, and he'd fix it up. I made it to his base, an hour outside Kansas City, and stayed the weekend. On Sunday morning, my sister called my brother. She had just moved to Rochester, Minnesota. After they chatted, I got on the call. We said our hellos, and I told her about school.

"Actually," said Suhair, "hang on. There's someone here you might want to speak with."

My brother and I assumed it was our little nephew, who at this point could say a few words. There were a few seconds of white noise on the other line.

DESTINED TO FAIL

"Hello?" a familiar voice breathed into the phone.

"*Mom*?"

She had arrived in the States that day to surprise us. We all planned to meet the next weekend, but I hadn't seen her in years. Elated, I said goodbye to my brother and flew to the car. I sped down the highway at ninety, shaving thirty minutes off a six-hour drive. My little VW hurtled over the Minnesota state line and screeched to a halt in front of my sister's new place.

When I burst inside unannounced, my brother-in-law's mouth fell open. Suhair exclaimed, "*Anas*!" I sank into my mom's arms and stayed there. Childhood flooded my senses; I was sixteen again. Life had been miserable, and seeing my mom again was the first time I had felt real joy in two years.

"How's Razi?" I asked.

My mom gave me the Jordan update. Then she asked, "What have you been up to?" I filled her in a little. An hour and a half passed.

"I have to go back to school," I announced, forlorn. "But I'll be back next weekend."

My mom clasped my hand and forearm as I made my way to the car. On the drive back, I thought about who I could convince to cover my shift next weekend. I wanted to spend it with my mom.

THE ACCOMPLISHMENT

In May 1996, my brother and sister, their families, and my mom drove down for my graduation. The ceremony was held at the Five Seasons Center, a giant concert venue in downtown Cedar Rapids. Graduating from an American college was the final milestone of what my parents expected of me. To the person I was three years ago, this day was unimaginable.

My mom and me at my graduation, 1996

DESTINED TO FAIL

When the school president called my name, I heard my mom holler. I walked over, a tassel in the corner of my eye, shook his hand, and received my diploma. The day felt limitless, like I had been released from a long prison sentence. *I'm done with school forever.* My hours of work and anxiety, with the added stress of academics, had paid off. I was proud of myself.

I had told my parents about Shanna during our phone calls. My mom then met her a few weeks prior to graduation, when she had just arrived in the States, and already liked her. Shanna was shy, but she had a sociable side that gave the impression that she was always happy to see you. My mom liked this about her. Shanna and I posed for a photo with my family in our graduation regalia.

The job search for dental technician positions, however, seemed futile. Betty, my dental lab instructor from Kirkwood, called me about open positions. When I was her student, she didn't like me. In school, I was often at work or sleeping instead of sitting for the morning lecture. I kept going to the interviews she sent me to, but whomever sat across from me would toss out my resume. Too young a face. Not enough experience.

One day, I was fed up.

"How did *you* start?" I asked an interviewer, a graduate of Kirkwood.

"I don't know. Someone took a chance on me." The irony was lost on him.

"You went to Kirkwood, right?"

He nodded.

"I did, too. Just graduated. Why don't you take a chance on me?"

The interviewer was silent.

That night, on the phone with Betty, she told me to go to an interview at a lab in Davenport. I was tired.

"I just want to be done." I sighed.

She persisted, and I finally agreed to go.

I drove an hour and a half from Cedar Rapids. I sat and waited for Bob, my interviewer, whom I heard shout at someone down the hall. When Bob came in, he picked up my resume and scanned it with beady eyes.

"Your resume looks like shit," he said.

"I don't have time for this," I said, flatly. I began to walk out.

"Wait," he said. "I think I could teach you something here."

Bob made his case. "I'll hire you for thirty days. It'll be a learning period. By day thirty, I'll tell you if you have the job."

I would have to drive every day for ninety minutes each way without knowing if this was a stable gig. It was a job making gold crowns for eight dollars an hour. I took it.

A month in, Bob approved the new hire. "You passed my test," he said. "You got a job here, kid. Go ahead and move to Davenport."

DESTINED TO FAIL

In December, Shanna and I moved to Davenport for a job I had scanned, cut, and pasted for. Shanna worked for a little while at a bank before she got a job in removables at a dental lab.

I established every aspect of working illegally the hard way. I filed my taxes and behaved as a legal citizen while in a strange illegal limbo. Fabricating documents became routine. Forgery was terrifying. Yet, once I learned the consequence was deportation, I began to fantasize of failing on purpose. In the days when my homesickness was most debilitating, this appealed to me. But I landed something I had worked toward and endured a lot for. I wouldn't let my dad see me fail.

I liked the feeling of following directions. Save for my slacking off in high school, I generally had a need to be obedient.

I racked my brain for a route out of the forgery. Marriage was the best I could think of. I never imagined my life would unfold as it did. I never wanted to get married, let alone at age twenty. I knew I was too young and didn't like the thought. But my situation warranted it. The feelings of disobedience and paralyzing fear would evaporate if I made things legal.

Citizenship aside, I really liked Shanna. She was kind in that salt-of-the-earth Midwestern sense. In my late teens and early twenties, I was adventurous and fun, but mostly, I was tough, because I had to be. I didn't have anyone else in my life, not even my friends, who acknowledged my heart. Shanna was the only person at the time who saw through that hard exterior.

"Hey," I said to her, "you wanna get married?"

"Okay." She shrugged. "Sounds good."

She didn't know about all the forged documents, but I explained to her that marriage would help with my legal status. She understood and agreed to it.

Shanna and I were legally married in Cedar Rapids. On December 14, we had a faux ceremony and a larger celebration in Decorah, Iowa. All of her family was there, and so were my friends from college, including Hani, my beloved Syrian friend. I thought of Carlos and missed him—I would have invited him had I known where to find him. That day, a snow storm swept the Midwest. Schools and highways shut down. Shanna and I got married when we were twenty, in the silent smothering of a blizzard.

The next time I saw my dad in person after being left at college was in Missouri. He had joined my mom in the Midwest, after liquidating everything back home: selling the house and the car and sorting out everyone's belongings. There was a family reunion, and it was my duty to go see him. I dreaded it.

For six hours in the car, I prepared myself mentally, like I had before every soccer game. *Go in there. Do your thing. Then get out*, I thought. My mind stretched, as it often did,

DESTINED TO FAIL

to every outcome. The questions he'd ask; the jabs he might make. *He's going to tell me what to do and how to do it. As if I'm still a kid.* The thought made me boil.

Over the last three years, I had operated as an adult. An overworked one, too. It wasn't that I was scared to see him. At seventeen, the most terrifying thing in my life had happened, and now I was afraid of everything and nothing. But I was anxious. *At the very least, I'll be cold,* I thought. *Like a businessman.* I was ready to fight if I had to. *Because some kind of conflict is inevitable.*

The house in Missouri was warm and smelled like my mom's cooking. I was glad she was there; her energy eased the animosity. Seeing my dad again was unremarkable. His tall tuft of hair had turned whiter. He no longer towered over me, but he was still intimidating.

I half-hugged him while I fixed my gaze on the ceiling. He asked how things were going, and I told him about the job in Davenport. During the reunion, with my family there, I used the house as a means to avoid the conflict. If my dad was downstairs, I stayed upstairs. Seeing him again for the first time since being dropped off at college didn't bring a rush of feeling. *This is just how it is now,* I thought.

Working in Iowa, I felt stunted. I was limited to one department, which stopped me from learning anything else. This interfered with the plans I had made in college.

"I'm starting my own lab before I'm twenty-three," I'd announced at age eighteen to Betty and a class of future dental technicians. Davenport itself was small and uninteresting. Since I was seventeen, I had dreamt of moving to Miami or Los Angeles, someplace warm and stimulating. Or glamorous New York or Chicago, for that matter. If I had to clench my gut in the cold some days, I would do it somewhere more exciting. I wasn't getting it from a town with nothing but a sad casino.

Early in 1997, I drove four hours from Davenport to visit Suhair and to iron out my citizenship application. She and her family had recently moved to Omaha, Nebraska from Rochester, Minnesota. I looked around the small city and saw a place where my life could expand. The people I met were kind. It was not ideal and it was perfectly cold in the winter. But compared to Davenport, Omaha felt big enough to get lost in.

U.S. Citizenship and Immigration Services took its sweet time to follow up. I had worked illegally, but in every other sense I followed the rules. I paid taxes and filed them on time.

In the plan to move from Davenport to Omaha, I changed my address with the state. I filled out the paperwork and scanned every detail of the form. I made sure everything looked all right and sent it out. An official letter from USCIS followed.

You are hereby notified to appear for an interview, it said.

DESTINED TO FAIL

Shanna and I drove to the main Office of Immigration and Naturalization for the Midwest, which happened to be in Omaha. We were separated and interviewed by different authorities.

Before we went in, I spoke with some friends about the interview. "Hopefully you don't get the bald guy," they said.

I waited in a small room in nervous silence. After a few minutes, a man entered. His bare scalp gleamed under the harsh fluorescents. He glared at me.

"I don't know where to begin with you," said the bald man. "There's no way you're not getting deported."

My mind raced. I tried to visualize the forms I'd filled out. *Where was the error?*

"You've been working illegally," he said, leaning on the words *federal crime.*

I swallowed.

"I'm not sure I've done anything wrong, sir. My employers were the ones who hired me. I pay my taxes every year. I'm a law-abiding citizen."

The bald officer towered over my chair and belittled me. As his tirade rolled on, I stared at the American flag pinned to his shirt pocket. He itched for me to put a toe out of line, so he could be the one to deport me.

"You will never see an American passport," the bald man said with a sneer.

My confusion had reached its apex and turned to irritation, but I restrained myself.

"Oh yes I will, sir," I replied. The bald man walked out.

After the interview, I stewed in fury over how he'd treated me. I debated with myself about what I could've said. *"Go ahead, deport me. You'd be doing me a favor."*

Back at the lab in Davenport, I noticed my colleague, Don, polishing something shiny.

"What's that?" I asked.

"It's a ring I made. I'm just polishing it up."

"You made that? Could you show me how?"

"Sure thing," he said.

I came down to the lab on weekends, and Don taught me the trade. We drove to Moline, a city ten minutes from Davenport. He showed me the gem store where he picked up his stones. My jewelry hobby evolved over time. I began to tinker away at rings of my own whenever I found a window in my schedule.

I was miserable at my job and sick of the Quad Cities. Davenport was depressing, and I hated several of my coworkers. I poured over the Omaha Yellow Pages and scored three interviews. They were all over the phone. The first was with Larsen Dental.

"How much experience do you have?"

"Two years."

A grunt of disapproval. "Can you do porcelain? We need someone who does porcelain."

DESTINED TO FAIL

"No, but I want to learn," I said.

They turned me down.

The other two labs both wanted to hire me. Southwest Dental paid a dollar more by the hour, so I accepted the offer. I told Shanna definitively that I wanted to move to Omaha. She said she had to run it by her dad. Naturally, her father disapproved; he didn't want her living so far from northeast Iowa. She always had to run things by him, which irked me.

"Well," I said, "I'm gonna go."

Finally, Shanna plucked up her courage, and her dad conceded. In September, we moved into an apartment complex in Omaha, Nebraska. My Green Card and legal status were sorted out in time.

The nomadic life I'd had as a child had made me comfortable moving from place to place, but Shanna struggled initially. She settled in when she got a job at a dental lab, one week after I began at Southwest Dental.

"Ace" was my nickname from Iowa, and it carried over into the new state. I began moving from one department to the next. I gained experience within each facet of the trade, including porcelain. My boss was an Air Force veteran, and my colleagues were hunters and fishermen who took me along on their expeditions. I established myself as an asset.

It didn't take long to realize how unqualified my boss was. His own work was crudely done. Anything the man touched, he destroyed. My coworkers and I had to redo the things he absent-mindedly tweaked. He was old, grizzled, and blind as a mole rat. And I was grossly underpaid.

Throughout my childhood, I'd had independence. When I arrived in the States, I found myself always working for somebody else, for many somebody elses, and it made me impatient.

Still, my ambition blazed. I fantasized about working at a lab where I was my own boss.

FEVER DREAM

Carlton was a traveling salesman. He sold dental alloys to labs out of a big, black briefcase. His territory was Iowa, Nebraska, Colorado, and Minnesota. I first met him at Kirkwood, where he demonstrated how to cast and solder.

In the first month of my job in Davenport, Carlton came into the lab. "Hey," he said. "This is where you're working?" He was a warm, good-natured elderly man with a refined taste in short-sleeve button-downs. By the time I moved to Omaha, Carlton and I were good friends.

"Everywhere I go, you follow me," I teased when he marched in with his wares. We began a tradition of meeting at Olive Garden whenever he was in town. It was his favorite.

One night, after a substantial dinner, we sat back in our chairs.

"Ready for dessert?" asked Carlton.

"I'm super-full," I said.

"No, you *need* the tiramisu," he said. I tried to refuse, but he explained the phenomenon. The espresso-soaked ladyfingers and mascarpone seemed too good to pass up.

I was hooked. He decided the two of us were a club. It was deemed the Tiramisu Club. I was a VIP member, and he appointed himself club president. I brought Shanna along sometimes, and she loved Carlton as much as I did.

When I turned twenty-two, the pressure set in. The prospect of starting my own business before age twenty-three was an ominous cloud over my head. I felt my father watching, criticizing every action from behind an imaginary door in my mind. I searched everywhere and managed to score some pieces of used equipment, but I was living paycheck to paycheck. My funds were lean.

In the spring of 1998, I had a conversation with Carlton.

"How the hell am I supposed to do this with no money?" I agonized.

"Come by my house Saturday," Carlton said. "I have something for you."

I drove two hours to Carlton's in Des Moines. The lab was connected to his house. As I pulled into the drive, he emerged. In each of his arms, he held a valuable piece of equipment.

"Pop your trunk," said Carlton. "Help me load this stuff."

My distress grew. *I can't afford this stuff. I can't pay him for it.*

DESTINED TO FAIL

When we finished loading the equipment, Carlton sighed.

"Olive Garden?" he asked, gleefully.

We scarfed down pasta and breadsticks and tiramisu.

As I nervously followed Carlton into the parking lot, I asked, "How much do I owe you?"

He shook his head. "I don't want anything," he said. "Start a lab. Do this for someone else someday."

Speech lodged in my throat as Carlton continued.

"Those two ounces of dental gold are usually seven hundred bucks. You can pay me back later."

I threw my arms around him.

"Thank you," I said, quietly.

During my time at Southwest, I met Dr. Greder, a dentist. He was a hardened veteran whose blue eyes bore into me as I worked. Besides polite greetings, we engaged in little conversation.

On one occasion, I overheard a conversation between him and my boss. "I get all my gold from Arizona," Dr. Greder said. "No one in Omaha does good enough work."

I knew how to make beautiful goldwork. It was the one thing I'd learned in Davenport from Bob. I got in the car in April 1999 and drove to the dentist's office. Dr. Greder's practice was in high demand, and the lobby was always busy. He beckoned me into his office.

"There isn't a dental technician in Omaha who does better goldwork than me," I told him.

Dr. Greder raised his eyebrows. "I'm picky," he said, tersely. "When are you up and running?"

"Right now," I said. "I'm not officially open, but give me a case. I'll do it for free, as a test."

Dr. Greder nodded. "I have one for you. I'll tell you how it seats."

In the spring of 1999, my small business was a humble station of production in my basement, the size of a modest bathroom. At that point, I only made gold crowns while at my full-time job at Southwest. In a conversation with Carlton over tiramisu, I asked him what he thought of Ace Dental Studio.

"Ace is my nickname. It's an A word, so it'll appear at the top of Yellow Pages."

Carlton approved, so I registered my business in May 1999.

Twenty days later, I turned twenty-three.

The phone rang with Dr. Greder on the other line.

"Come see me in my office," he directed. It was a summons not unlike the kind my dad would issue when I was a child. I drove over. *Am I in trouble?*

The receptionist approved my entry into the dentist's office. Dr. Greder offered me reserved congratulations.

"This is one of the nicest gold cases I've seen."

DESTINED TO FAIL

I reached out my hand. "No more Phoenix?" I asked.

"No more Phoenix." Dr. Greder chuckled.

We agreed I would do all of Dr. Greder's goldwork.

"I'm young, but I'm old-fashioned," I said. "I just shake hands."

In the summer of 1999, I went to a pool party at my next-door neighbor's house in Omaha. In a moment on my own, I gravitated toward the soccer ball lying in the yard. I made two futile attempts to punt it into a basketball hoop hanging over the pool and finally scored.

"You play soccer?" a young man asked.

"A little," I said.

"Are you any good?"

"I haven't played in years."

"Well, if you ever wanted to play," the young man offered, "we've got a team, and we're short on guys." The young man introduced himself as Bill.

I took him up on it. There were specific shoes I had to buy for indoor soccer. I hadn't run or jumped in four years, and I worried about my stamina. *Hope my lungs hang in there.*

I arrived at the first game of the season, and Bill introduced me to the other players. He explained the slightly different rules of indoor soccer. One of the players approached me and introduced himself as Tony.

"Where are you from?" he asked.

"Jordan," I said.

"Are you sure you're not from Cuba?" Tony giggled.

Cuba? I looked at him funny.

"You look like Manny from *Scarface*. Anyone ever tell you that?"

I laughed. "No, I never heard that one."

Tony asked me what position I played, and I told him I was a forward. "All I know is how to score goals. I could never play defense or midfield."

"That's exactly what this team is missing," Tony said. "Stay up top, and shred that goalie."

The whistle sounded, and the game began. On defense, Tony was relentless. His feet drew closer, and I ran to intercept the ball. I thought I'd be rusty, but my muscles remembered. I punted the ball over the goalie's futile dive.

I hadn't scored a goal in years and couldn't contain myself. I sprang into the air. The game went on, and I scored again twice. For each one, I paraded about as if we'd won the World Cup. The sensation was fresh. The team won 5-2. The new kid had made all the difference, and the players were impressed.

Tony congratulated me. "Great game, dude!" He leaned in. "Maybe tone it down a bit on the celebrations though," he said.

"I'll work on it." I laughed. "But I can't promise anything."

Tony and I stood around and talked for a while after the game. We exchanged phone numbers. The next game was as successful as the first. The team played hard, I scored a few goals, and we won.

Tony and I went fishing one Saturday and discovered we had multitudes in common. I could see Tony was different. He was olive-skinned, too, and steeped in a culture deeper than the one around us. He had grown up in an immigrant household. Although we hailed from different countries, we'd endured the same kinds of hardships. A competitive streak and a deep love for soccer were our common denominators.

Me (as Manny from Scarface) *and Tony dressed for Halloween*

In that first month, we talked every day. At 10 a.m., Tony had a break at work, and he'd call me. We went on for fifteen minutes about everything or nothing in particular. When I finally watched *Scarface*, we devoted the first five minutes to quoting it. I hadn't talked to anyone that often since Mustafa.

A month after the fishing trip, we went to a burger joint. I ordered, and Tony asked the important question for me.

"Hey, is there pork on that?"

We were Tony and Manny. Our relationship was that of two siblings. Each would drop everything to help the other.

I became the common-law fourth child of Tony's family. Tony's parents, Benny and Lucia, were Italian immigrants. They were part of an established Italian community on the south side of Omaha that had forged the railroads a hundred years before.

Benny and I were the tough immigrant breadwinners; we scraped by and struggled and triumphed. We had come here barely understanding a word of the language. He and I mirrored each other. Before he retired, he'd worked three jobs, where I currently worked two jobs that felt like three. Benny saw his younger self in me: hardworking and ambitious. I saw my future in Benny.

Playing soccer

Tony and I played a few times a week on the indoor soccer team. Tony pressed his friend, Maurizio, the coach of an outdoor team in Omaha, to consider me. "You *have* to get this guy on your team."

I hadn't played on an outdoor team since college. My average was two goals a game. I was glad to play in the elements again, on real grass and in the crisp air.

Over the next year, I worked at Southwest Dental during the day. At night, I hunched over my workstation, making gold crowns in a dimly lit basement. In the span of the year, Ace Dental made $9,067.12. I saved it all.

The real money was not in gold, however, but in porcelain crowns. Although I had some equipment from Carlton, it was still insufficient. The annual Midwinter Dental Meeting was a national convention for dentists and dental labs in Chicago that promised good deals and high-quality equipment. In February 2000, I went to the bank. Against my good sense, I approached the clerk and nervously cleared my throat. I told her I wanted to empty all but five dollars from my business and personal accounts.

On the seven-hour drive to Chicago, I desperately played Metallica to drown out my terror. In the evening, the city rose up from Lake Michigan. I spent all my money on supplies and equipment and bit my nails on the drive home.

In late-winter 2000, drifts of snow turned to ice and sediment at the side of the road. I argued with my boss. The equipment from the trip to Chicago, including a casting machine and a torch from Carlton, was set up and in use.

Rebecca began as a new employee. She made porcelain crowns. She worked at Southwest, too, until I spoke with her about working at Ace. My boss knew about the deal with Dr. Greder. He shook his fists in indignation: I was indispensable, and he couldn't afford to fire me.

The first week in March, I sat on my bench at Southwest Dental. I had benefits and insurance, and the paycheck was steady. But I was paid fifteen dollars an hour.

I sat, tranquil, hands by my side, gazing at the entirety of my work.

I do all of this, I thought. *To be told what to do by an unqualified person for fifteen dollars an hour. And how much could I make myself?*

At the end of the meditation, I sighed. I wriggled the key from the chain and set it on my boss's desk. In the parking lot, a weight crashed from my shoulders onto the pavement. I didn't worry. I soaked up the late winter sun on my face.

The same day, I called Dr. Greder. "I can do porcelain crowns," I said.

He accepted the offer. He had a case for me. Rebecca and I did our part and sent it out.

Dr. Greder called me in a week's time. "Stop by my office," he said.

When I arrived, the doctor greeted me.

"I want you to run an in-house lab in my office," he said. "Bring your equipment."

There was space for Rebecca and me, and the two of us worked out of the dentist's basement. This was a huge opportunity: we knew how much work they did, and it would all come straight to us. The needs of the patients, which always overwhelmed Dr. Greder's lobby, inundated us downstairs. Usually, I was accustomed to producing two crowns a day. Now the demand was ten to fifteen. My two-person team rushed to keep up. I was swept into the rhythm of demand: case after case after case. I stopped getting a good night's sleep, but our income grew substantially. We multiplied by twenty what we had made formerly in a month. I was grateful for my instinct.

Shanna and I discussed her taking on an administrative position at my dental lab. She liked the idea, since it meant she could leave her other job. Soon, she began working as the bookkeeper. We agreed that she'd handle the business and I'd handle the production. Neither of us had been to business school or accounting classes or knew how QuickBooks worked. We learned on the job. My work was grueling. On occasion, I peered over her shoulder and could see how the business and accounting end was equally perplexing.

Shanna told me she was pregnant just as the cornfields were succumbing to frost. As I thought about it, I was excited to be a dad—I had always wanted to have two kids, a boy and a girl. Yet I was young, still learning to set a boundary between work and home. To have gotten my business off the ground and struggled under the burden of it was one thing. The prospect of fatherhood was another, an uncharted territory I wasn't sure I was prepared for.

I was twenty-four years old, but in my heart, I was still seventeen. I didn't feel like a father. I thought perhaps I'd be somewhat larger and wealthier than who I was at the moment, by the time I was prepared for a child. My childhood vacations were spent picking wildflowers in the French countryside. I was lucky enough to have a childhood of travel, where I saw places like Paris and Cairo. I worried I wouldn't be able to provide my child with the great experiences given to me.

Shanna was kind. I liked being around her for the most part. Our relationship was tolerable, but our arguments were frequent and petty. The anxiety I experienced daily made me too self-absorbed to support and consider my wife. At twenty-four, I lacked the maturity to ask after her wellbeing. There were all sorts of demands on my plate: a deadline every minute, a short-staffed business, and a lack of sleep. I was still trying to juggle it all. Because of this, I didn't give Shanna the attention I gave to my work.

As time progressed, my angry outbursts grew more regular. Shanna saw more of them than anyone. "Why do you get so angry?" she would ask.

At the time, I wasn't entirely aware.

Tony had me over one day to play FIFA on his original PlayStation. We sat on the couch, where I always played Spain and Tony played Italy. They were the best two teams.

"For laughs," Tony said, "you play Jordan, and I'll play Lebanon." Jordan and Lebanon were the worst.

"Sure," I said. The characters were all real athletes on professional leagues who played on a national level. We went through our respective players. Then, I looked up from the controller, and my face fell.

A boy I played soccer with on Coach Ibrahim's team stared back at me from Tony's TV.

"What's up?" asked Tony.

"That player." I pointed to the screen. "I used to be on a team with him. Back in Jordan."

I remembered Ibrahim, the only adult who saw my potential as a professional athlete. I recalled the giddy feeling on the bus after I'd been recruited. The dream of my sixteen-year-old self that had been silenced. The phone call to Ibrahim that I never made swam about in the void. I had watched professional soccer recede further. One year had melted into five and five into ten.

DESTINED TO FAIL

In another life, it could have been my shiny face on Tony's PlayStation. I looked at my former teammate. *Look at me!* his eyes whispered. *I'm living my dream!*

All through my twenties, reminders like these upset me. My athletic prime was being wasted here, sitting still, hunched over my uninspired job.

My chest fell as reality sank in.

In June 2001, my neighbors invited me on a four-day fishing trip to Canada, along with their teenage sons. They were men fifteen or more years my senior.

I had received a letter in June 1998 that deemed me a lawful, permanent resident. During my five years living in the United States, I had been in an anxious limbo: *can't work, need money, break rules, worry.* The relief was immense.

Following the first statement, the letter went on to say that I would need to obtain a new Alien Registration Receipt Card (it had a depressing little code: Form I-551) and appear in person with two forms of ID. They told me they'd send the receipt six months later, and I was not permitted to travel internationally until it arrived.

But Immigration & Naturalization hadn't followed up in three years. I had no Alien Registration Receipt Card, no Green Card, and no U.S. passport. There was no documentation to prove their lack of contact.

I talked to Shanna about going on the trip. She was due in thirty days. This was a lot to ask of a woman about to have her first baby, but eventually she agreed I should go. The thought of a drawn-out detainment in Canada was petrifying yet short-lived.

I decided to go anyway.

We were all in good spirits for the drive north. My next-door neighbor, Rick, drove us up I-80 from Omaha, through Des Moines and Minneapolis and Duluth. The van smelled of sweat and earth. We stopped to stretch our legs on the prairie, grasses hopping with hind-legged insects and gardener snakes.

The fishing trip took place on a remote island on Lake Superior. Accessible only by floatplane, it required multiple trips back and forth to accommodate everyone and their things. Once the floatplane finished its rounds, we were warned not to clean fish near the cabin, because it would attract the grizzly bears. The survival kit under the sink had nothing but four sheets.

"Oh, it's to spell out *H-E-L-P*," one of my neighbors observed.

The pilots circled over us in the mornings and afternoons. They would see our signal, if a disaster occurred.

Our catch was abundant, mostly northern pike and walleye. Around us, stunted trees and moss clung to formidable cliffs. Deep-green pines grew, massive and girthy. I caught sight of a moose, his antlers magnifying his awesome stature, as he gnawed on some overhanging branches.

After four days, we piled into the van again with our catch. My chest tightened as the car neared the border, and my heart rate quickened. Customs rolled into view, where German Shepherds were harnessed to scowling men with beady eyes. The patrol officer, a woman with blonde hair yanked into a low bun, approached the van. She stuck her head through the driver's window.

"Purpose of your visit?" she barked.

"Just going home, ma'am. Father-son fishing trip," said Rick.

She nodded her head. "I'm opening the side door," she said. I was face-to-face with her.

She asked another passenger before she asked me, "Are you an American citizen?"

"Yes ma'am."

The patrol officer asked every passenger. Some officers checked the fish for Canadian trailer-park meth. The officer met her quota.

"Welcome home, boys," she said.

I closed my eyes and melted into the seat.

When I returned from Canada, I threw myself into work again. I overcompensated to save up for the time off to see my child born. Shifts stretched on unbearably long, sometimes for thirty hours, at which time I gave myself two hours of shuteye. My brain wandered.

In my sleepless delirium, Shanna called and said she was going into labor. I sped home, and we drove to the Methodist Hospital.

Shanna was helped onto the seventh floor, into a room tucked in the corner. Her good friend Cora arrived a little later, and while she and the nurses situated my wife, I felt overwhelmed by my severe exhaustion. I took advantage of a recliner. As Shanna wailed and calculated her breaths, I fell in and out of sleep, unable to discipline a body that desperately needed rest. The fluorescent lights of the maternity ward seemed to fade in and out of my vision. For twenty-seven hours, Shanna labored.

Nader means "unique" in Arabic. My son was born in the morning, as an endless June 30 faded into July 1. My consciousness plastered itself to the ceiling, and I watched the birth from above, as if in a fever dream. There was commotion all around the baby's emerging, yet we didn't hear him cry. Nader was born in silence, the cord wrapped around his neck. Shanna and I watched, wide-eyed, as several nurses rushed over with a cart. For forty-five seconds, they worked on him until he let out a scream. We all heaved sighs of relief and joy.

When I held the infant, the awe hit me on top of the exhaustion. *I'm a dad,* I thought, although the truth of this baby being my own didn't hit me until much later.

DESTINED TO FAIL

It had been two days of no sleep, so I napped again, exhausted. When I woke up, Shanna reminded me I had to let the dog out. I drove home, and opened the door so Abby, our Labrador, could do her business in the yard. My head spun. She trotted back inside, tail wagging. I took a few steps into the house and collapsed on the floor. I called Shanna at the hospital.

"Something's really wrong," I said. "I'm gonna pass out."

Shanna sent for Rick, our six-foot-four neighbor. He appeared in three minutes. Heroically towering over me at the threshold, he asked if I was all right. Then, Rick helped me into the car, and we drove to the same hospital.

I lay in the ER, while my wife and newborn son were seven floors above me.

"Why do you think you're feeling like this?" the doctor asked.

"I haven't slept in forty-eight hours," I said.

"Well, of course you're falling over and passing out," he said, then nimbly injected something into my forearm.

I fell into a deep sleep. In the interval when I was awake, they wheeled my bed upstairs next to my wife. I slept the whole night.

I watched Nader grow, and it melted me. When he was a baby, I'd sit with his butt in the palm of my hand and stare at his sleeping face. All of his little movements thrilled me.

Yet his existence was confounding. *Is this really my baby?* It wasn't until he formed words, like *Mama* and *Daddy*, that it began to dawn on me: he was mine.

Baby Nader

Nader and me

DESTINED TO FAIL

After Nader was born, I continued to play soccer with Tony. It was only when we met that I had rediscovered the game. I had given up on my dreams. *This is my life now,* I had said to myself.

Tony's friendship was a blessing. The joy I had known as an athlete returned.

My parents had never been to any of my soccer games. I had always longed for their support, but throughout my childhood I was conditioned to never expect it, since they would never approve. As a kid, each time I scored a goal, I looked to the sidelines and imagined they were there. My mind created two holograms where they stood, my mom cheering and waving, my dad nodding in solemn approval.

My parents had become permanent residents of the U.S. in the mid-nineties. When I was twenty-six, they came to visit Nader in Omaha. We were all at the house when I gathered my things for a Thursday soccer game. My parents, occupied with the newborn, looked up to see me on my way out the door.

"Where are you going?" they asked.

"A soccer game," I said. "You wouldn't want to come, would you?"

To my disbelief, they both said yes.

I was always quiet before a game. I imagined every outcome, from wins to losses to ties. With my parents in the backseat, I only pictured wins. *I'm gonna score thirty goals,* I thought. *Then, Dad's gonna announce he's taking me back to Jordan to try out for the national team. Because then, he'll realize I'm worth it.*

I'm not a failure. He'll see.

I was a beast on the field that day, slamming bodies and scoring goals. My parents' presence was my incentive to demolish the other team. We vanquished the opposition. When I looked over at the sidelines, the figures of my parents were imaginary no more. I half expected them to be gazing obsessively at Nader. But they stood there, attentive. My mom clapped and jumped up and down when something exciting happened. My dad, though never as expressive as my mom, was intensely focused on the game. I was surprised by how engaged he was, even in his own stoic way.

Tony knew a little about the fraught relationship between me and my dad. After the game, my parents filed out of the stands. My mom smiled at me and flung her arms wide open. Tony approached my dad.

"He's pretty damn good, isn't he?" Tony said, in solidarity.

"Yes," said my dad, unsmiling. "Yes, he is."

I knew he was proud of me. To see him there thrilled and hurt me all at once. He was the one who had torn my potential from me.

DESTINED TO FAIL

Of course, the fantasy never came to fruition. After their visit, he and my mom would go back to Missouri. But he was present, at least. I didn't want the moment to end.

On May 9, 2002, I had an easy day at work. Afterward, I drove over to the soccer field. The sky was clear. There was little wind, and the air was mild. The team had a regular season game.

I ran up the field and spotted Val, a brilliant twenty-one-year-old forward from Cameroon, in his bright orange shoes. Everybody wore grays, blacks, and whites, and the team liked to poke fun at him for his cutting-edge fashion.

I made a long-distance pass to the bright-orange shoes. Val scored. We were winning at half time, when I caught up with him.

"Thanks for that assist," he said.

"How can I miss you with those on?" I joked. "I can see you from all the way across the field."

Val took it in stride. We sprinted onto the pitch. I occupied my usual position on offense. I was sure the opposition was done for, and I was right. Our team upheld our winning streak.

Halfway into the second half, Maurizio subbed me out. We were on cruise control now; there was no urgent need for the goal-scorer. I sat on the bench and caught my breath, watching from the sidelines.

Val ran forward. He tripped and fell, face first. He didn't put his hands out to stop himself. I watched him, and he didn't spring back up. *Something's wrong,* I thought.

The men close to Val ran over and crouched. They flipped him over and began to frantically wave.

"He needs CPR!" one of them shouted. I rose from the bench and joined the men huddled around our teammate. Val was unmoving.

Faces fell blank. No one knew what to do. I kneeled and performed CPR.

An eternity passed, and I neared dizziness before a hand moved my head out of the way. Tony administered his breath until the ambulance arrived. As the paramedics rolled out the stretcher, Tony, Maurizio, our friend Brad, and I grabbed our belongings and bolted to the car.

When the four of us arrived at the hospital, a receptionist who recognized our uniforms pointed us down the hall. The doctor opened the door to the room. His face was solemn.

"You're his teammates?" he asked. We nodded. "Your friend has expired. I'm sorry."

A moment of disbelief prevented the truth from setting in.

"What do you mean?" we said. "He's twenty-one."

"He's passed. I'm sorry."

The four of us looked at one another. "We can't leave him."

DESTINED TO FAIL

As we stood rooted to the floor outside Val's hospital room, a woman burst through the doors. My stomach dropped. It was Val's mother. The doctor took her aside and spoke to her in low tones. The woman let out a wail. She ran into the room and screamed. My hair stood on end.

My friends and I were ushered into the room. The boy was lifeless, his clothes torn during the futile attempts to revive him. My eyes locked on his orange shoes. *We were just out there, playing soccer,* I thought.

For a long time, the four of us were stunned, unable to move. *We can't just leave our teammate.* Eventually, someone had to escort us out. That night, I thought of Val's mother's screams. Shanna sat by me for a while and comforted me. I held Nader and didn't let him go.

Val had an enlarged heart. He was pronounced dead on arrival, but the doctor said he was gone before he hit the grass. The funeral was awful. I still couldn't emote, but the devastation there was enough to make me feel.

The following game was on a Thursday. Maurizio gathered both teams together. We bowed our heads and prayed.

Whenever I played on the same field, I stood where Val fell and sprinkled the spot with a silent prayer. I hated playing on that field. I had seen dislocated shoulders and broken legs, but I'd never thought I would see a heart give out.

A YEAR AND A HALF

In the late nineties and early 2000s, Omaha experienced an influx in its population. The locals, although city folk in theory, were averse to living in tall buildings and tight quarters. They were Midwesterners at heart who wanted to spread out and live comfortably in a big house with a garage and a generous lawn. While the economy was still good, a number of people moved to a more residential section on the west side of the city.

Shanna and I were among the masses. I scouted a few neighborhoods. Carlo, a good friend of mine, lived in West O. His son, Gino, was nine days younger than Nader.

"You should move to this neighborhood," Carlo said. "Then our boys can grow up together."

Shanna and I decided to build a house there. In Jordan, houses are heirlooms of familial importance, permanent fixtures to be passed down through generations. I dedicated myself to its construction every day for seven months. By the end, it was three times the size of our first house; a welcome addition to the landscaped suburban neighborhood.

The birth of my second child was reasonably calculated. On February 1, I received a call at work. I knew to bring the hospital bag. The only turmoil erupted from the clouds, which were dense with wintry particles. An ice storm battered the windows as I drove my wife to the hospital.

I dropped Shanna at the entrance, where she was helped inside, and parked the truck in the garage directly across from the hospital. As I crossed the street, I looked up at the small stretch of open sky, which was spitting ice. *Please God,* I prayed. *Let it be a girl.*

Fourteen-degree winds whistled outside the same hospital room in the corner where Nader was born. Over the course of Shanna's pregnancy, she and I decided we didn't want to know the gender of the baby. I had wanted to be a daddy to a little girl, to have that experience.

Danah, a name meaning "rare pearl" in Arabic, was born in the evening.

"It's a girl!" the doctor exclaimed over her screams. The nurses cleaned her up, wrapped her in a blanket, and stuck a little hat on her head. They handed her to me. I cried tears of happiness as I held my beautiful baby girl.

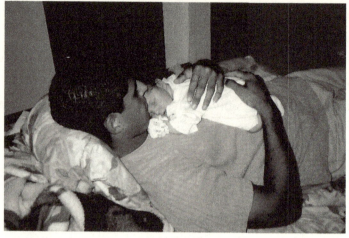
Baby Danah

In the time between my arrival to the States and the day my first child was born, my capacity for feeling had grown significantly smaller. In my late teens and early twenties, I felt as if nobody cared about me—I lacked support and safety, and this darkened my whole mindset. *If nobody cares about me*, I thought, *why should I care about anybody else?* I carried this naïve, selfish apathy into my relationships and into my marriage. So, my heart didn't sing when I thought of my wife or my work. Even Jordan wasn't dear to me anymore.

With Nader in my arms, though, the love rushed in, and the bitterness subsided a little. Then, Danah softened my heart. Fatherhood was a different kind of love, one that forced my hard self to break open. Soon, the block of cinders was no more, and I had a beating heart again.

DESTINED TO FAIL

Me and my babies

The birth of my kids changed the relationship between Shanna and me. As a new father, my heart expanded. I loved Shanna—she was the mother of my beautiful children. All I wanted to do with my time was work to provide for my family's financial comfort. Over time, I would become obsessive about it. Although it stemmed from a fear of failure, it was out of love.

In the summer of 2005, I moved Ace Dental out of Dr. Greder's basement and bought a former dental office on the southwest side of town. Dr. Harley, a dentist, had set up shop there in 1960 and retired some time ago. The place had sat vacant for years. Tony and his dad, Benny, helped me tear out the old carpeting, paint the walls, and clear out the overgrown backyard. They arrived in the morning and helped me long into the night.

"Go home, Mr. Buccheri," I said to Benny. "You've done plenty!"

"Forget it," said Tony. "He's stubborn!"

Benny hated when I called him *Mister* and reproached me for it. He slid a thumb across his neck, amusement in his eyes. In two days, with their help, the place looked sharp and smelled of fresh, white paint.

Tony's folks, Benny and Lucia, lived a few blocks away from the new dental lab. I dropped by for an occasional coffee with my new Italian "parents," and chatted with Benny. Often, Benny walked to the lab, and I made him coffee. For the twenty minutes Benny sat with me, work halted, no matter what was due.

Benny called me *ananas,* which in Italian meant pineapple, and it tickled him to no end. When he got up to leave, he teased me. "You never come to visit me," he said, a twinkle in his eye. "If you don't come see me, I'll slash your tires." The joke never got old.

A year into working in the new building, I began to hear noises late at night. Floorboards creaked. Vacuums revved on their own accord. Lights blinked on and off, and a key left in the lock would turn $360°$ by itself. There was a ghost in the lab. I was sure of it. My employees heard noises and felt presences, too. No one dared to work late, because they were afraid of an encounter. I never feared the ghost. I named him Harvey, an indirect nod to the dentist before me.

In fall 2008, I got a strange call from a man who called himself Freddy. Freddy owned a dental lab in Des Moines. He said he wanted me to make a frame, a metal substructure used for porcelain work. I thought he was crazy and refused. I was too busy, and I didn't work for other labs.

"They told me you're the best," Freddy insisted. "And it's an important case. It's for the doctor's wife!"

"Sorry, man. Go find someone else," I said and hung up.

A few days went by, and Freddy called again. "I'm putting it in the mail!" said Freddy. "You'll get it tomorrow!"

Whatever. I made the frame anyway. When Freddy received it in the mail, he called me.

"This is the best! You're gonna do *all* my frames!" I reiterated that I didn't work for other labs, plus I was way too busy.

Freddy scoffed. "Why are you so stubborn? Where are you from?" When I told him, Freddy said he was Lebanese. He cussed me out in Arabic, and I lit up in amusement. We began to talk daily for hours on end. With time, we became close friends.

Shanna had wanted to be a stay-at-home mom until both of our kids were old enough to go to school. I thought it would be good for them to grow up with their mom around. When Nader was an infant, she'd bring him in to see me work. Shanna was a good mom. She was sensitive and nurturing, a present and loving figure to our children.

Our social lives were large and vibrant. Around the time of Nader's birth, Shanna and I befriended a woman named Shelley, an insurance agent. She was our age, and Shanna and I spent time with her. Shelley and I would go out for lunch or Shanna would see her for drinks. Sometimes, we all went out together.

Over the next four years, Ace took off. As I got busier with work, the two women became best friends. I set up my business account at a bank, where I met a friendly man named Paul. He had a young family like mine. We had many dinners together with our wives and children.

I didn't sleep. Work was like a riptide, sucking me out to sea. The only solution was to surrender. On weekdays, my shifts went on for ten hours. I would always eat dinner at home and sometimes help Shanna put our kids to bed. Then, around nine in the evening, I would drive back to work for the graveyard shift. At four or five in the morning, I would drive home and sleep, then at 7:00 or 8:00, I would drive back to work again. On weekends, my shift might have gone on for thirty-five hours straight.

During those long shifts, Shanna would come to the lab with the kids and bring me dinner.

DESTINED TO FAIL

Nader and Danah, ages 5 and 3

Ace Dental was understaffed; there were only three other employees. To endure the spine-crunching workload, we would need three more. Sometimes, when the hours of sleep were too few or the workload grew unmanageably heavy, I cried in a deep, instinctive way that made no sense to me. I didn't realize how overwhelmed I was.

Even amid a hectic work life, the income was a relief. Minimum wage and food-service jobs were well behind me. I didn't have to struggle for nice things anymore. I bought a sleek new car. In that span of time, I embraced my love for cars and went through several in rapid succession. With the comfort of a swift growth, I didn't think about the Ace Dental business account. I had an idea of what came in, but Shanna was the bookkeeper, and I left that part to her.

While Ace Dental skyrocketed, Shanna wanted for nothing, and her spending habits were reasonable. Her concern was making sure the kids had nice things. She was big on Christmas, and I could gauge how well Ace had done that year by the size of the stack of presents.

Shanna and the kids were comfortable, but I never stopped going. Life never levelled. Ace was making a lot of money, but nothing satisfied me. When I'd arrived in the States, I'd programmed myself to think that working until your back gave out was normal. I was never sentimental about how far I'd come. There was a tiny drill sergeant in my mind constantly shouting *"Go! Go! Go!"* and he had real power over me. To satiate that inner critic always required my foot on the gas.

When I wasn't working, I thought about it obsessively; I couldn't sit still. Over the years, it became therapeutic, because that's how I sought purpose—it was for my children, to build their future. And, to prove I wasn't a failure.

Shanna drove the kids to see her parents in northeast Iowa several times a year. I always tried to make Christmas on the farm, but December had a way of sweeping me up in work, and this year was particularly busy. I couldn't make Christmas or Easter.

Our relationship suffered. I was always present for my kids, for their assemblies and sporting events, and I gave them whatever they needed. But the business was everything. I was so preoccupied with the need to provide that I thought even less about my marriage than before.

However, even with my exhausted, preoccupied brain, I saw something in Shanna shift. Her low-cut blouses and bright shades of lipstick caught my eye as she rushed out the door. She joined a gym for the first time. Our bedroom life grew stale.

As the year rolled on, a notion sprouted in my mind. I confided in Rebecca.

"I think Shanna's having an affair."

"No!" Rebecca chuckled. "She would never."

Everyone thought of Shanna as an angel. They weren't wrong: she was sweet and kind-spoken. Though I was always outgoing, by my early thirties I was a loudmouth who could be short-tempered and prickly. I had also become narrow-minded, petty, and intensely competitive with myself. Immediately, Rebecca's words seeped into my consciousness and became my motive. It didn't mean much to me if Shanna was seeing someone else. My affection had been diluted by years of survivor's mentality. All I wanted was to prove to myself that my instinct was right.

But what if it's one of my friends? I was worried at that thought. I came up with three suspects, all of whom were men married to her friends. I guessed the passwords to her email account. Finally, I hacked it and scoured her inbox. It was empty of personal exchanges.

There's no way she would go three days without getting anything. Emails were being deleted.

Shanna and I appeared to be a handsome, happy, accomplished couple with our angelic children playing in the front yard. But the dynamic in the house had shifted. Over the last year, Shanna had started to pay me less attention. I could tell she was annoyed when I'd come home. While the kids were loved and doted on by her, I started to feel, at best, as if I was her roommate. At worst, I felt like a cash register. *How did we get here?* I thought. *Why is she changing? And why won't she talk to me?*

My gut told me the marriage was over. Perhaps foolishly, I waited for something to fall through on its own. Or for Shanna to call it like it was. I was so caught up with work, I didn't make the initiative.

There was a lady, the office manager at a dental office I worked for, who winked whenever I passed the desk. She aggressively flirted with me, and I reciprocated. Our conversations grew personal, and she told me about her own disintegrating marriage. Soon, I was happy to see her. We helped each other through our respective marriage struggles. One day, we started fooling around. I communicated with her through email and whenever I saw her in person.

Shanna's lies grew transparent as the year went on. One day in April, I called her, and she didn't pick up. I thought she was supposed to drive the kids home from school. On the thirtieth ring, she answered. She said something, but it was unintelligible. *Shanna's having a stroke,* I thought. Panicked, I got in the car and raced home at a hundred and ten miles per hour.

The kids were there; they had caught the bus. I let out a sigh of relief. *They're fine.*

"Where's Mom?" I asked.

"She's upstairs," Nader said. "She's sick."

I walked into our room where I found Shanna, hammered.

"You're not just sick," I said, fuming. "You're drunk."

"No, really, I'm just sick," she slurred. "Food poisoning or something."

I had been around enough to know what drunk looked like. Shanna was so inebriated, I didn't know how she'd made it home. She reeked of liquor, too.

That night, she lay in our room with the door closed. I made sure the kids ate dinner and went to sleep. The next morning ready for school. Shanna was sitting up in bed. *I have to talk to her about what happened. But I can't get too angry.*

"You can't fool me with your food-poisoning bullshit," I said. "I know you were smashed." Despite my intention to remain calm and mature, I erupted. I screamed, "Don't *ever* let my kids see you like that!"

Shanna had grown immune to my frequent outbursts. She lay back down and shifted away from me. I closed the door to the room and drove the kids to school. I was scared for them, but I had to go to work. My instincts about her solidified.

I got home from the lab one day in the fall of 2009. I looked out the window facing the backyard, where Shanna paced back and forth on the phone. She had walked as far from the house as possible so no one could hear the conversation. I thought that was odd. A few minutes later, I heard her come inside. I was sitting in the bedroom when Shanna marched in and threw several sheets of paper at me in self-righteous anger.

She shouted her accusation at me. "Cheater!"

The papers were the notes the office manager and I had written to each other. Shanna was hacking emails, too. She printed everything out. I denied cheating on her. At this point, I was almost certain that she was cheating, too. But that self-competitive streak kicked in: she was winning the fight. *I don't have anything on her,* I thought.

Later, Shanna told me she had been on the phone with her father when I'd seen her in the backyard. She told both her parents and Shelley that I was unfaithful. Perhaps she told others, too. Shanna was sweet and kind, and everyone stuck to her honey. Nobody would believe me, if I told them otherwise.

From then on, our marriage truly ceased to function. Shanna and I barely spoke to each other. She avoided me. When we were in the same room, she had an air of discomfort. I slept on the couch in the basement, so I wouldn't have to sleep next to her. Our sex life was nonexistent. If I died in a car wreck, she'd have worn red to my funeral.

A few weeks later, Shanna stopped by the lab. Her eyes glinted. The perfume on her collarbone wafted through the office. Everyone looked up. On some level, they all knew.

"Where are you going?" I asked.

"The bank," she said, eyes lowered.

Under the pretense of our failing marriage, I asked Shanna if she wanted to go on an anniversary trip to Kansas City. I had nothing to lose. There was proof of my infidelity, but hers was only in theory. I wanted to put some effort into my marriage, for the kids' sakes at least.

"Our personal life is a disaster," I said. "And our anniversary is coming up. Why don't we put everything aside and leave town for a weekend? Maybe that's what we need to restart our marriage."

To my surprise, she agreed. "That sounds good," she said. "Let's go to Kansas City."

She booked a hotel. I set everything aside when we got in the truck, and we talked for most of the drive. During that weekend in December, we forgot about our lives back in Omaha. I stopped speculating, and Shanna became quietly effervescent again. College and our spontaneous late-teens came rushing back. We talked and laughed.

Maybe we should make this thing work, I thought on the drive home.

Monday the fourteenth was our anniversary. When I came home from work that day, Shanna was on the verge of tears but wouldn't tell me why.

A week passed. Three days before Christmas, her heels clicked on the hard tiles of the dental lab. She was there for thirty minutes.

"I've gotta go," Shanna announced and gathered her things.

"Where are you going?" I asked.

"Bank," she said. "For a meeting."

Her manicured fingernails curled around the door handle. A rush of cold air hit me as the door opened. Something dormant in my gut sprang alive. It made perfect sense.

Our friend, Paul, the banker.

She would be at the bank in ten minutes, I figured, so I raced to the computer and logged into her email account. I impatiently hit the computer screen as Hotmail loaded slowly. Paul had never been one of my suspects. Then, two emails appeared at the top of her inbox.

I love you, Paul the banker had typed.

I love you, too, Shanna had replied. *What we have is very special.*

I printed the emails and walked over to Rebecca at her bench.

"See?"

Rebecca took the copy in her hands and read the emails twice. Her jaw dropped.

Five minutes passed. Shanna was on the road by then, so I called her.

"When you get to the bank, wait for me," I said. "I'll meet you there."

"Why?" she asked.

"Don't call anyone else." I hung up.

My eyes were on the clock as I put on my coat. When a minute had passed, I called her again.

"You called him," I said, just to catch her off guard.

She stuttered on the other line.

"If you wait there," I said, "things will be peaceful."

When I arrived at the bank, Shanna was parked out front. I walked over to her SUV, and got in on the passenger's side. I was still in a spell of disbelief. This was Shanna; I *knew* her. We'd been married for thirteen years. We had two kids together. I wouldn't believe it unless I heard the words come out of her mouth.

I looked over at her.

"I know what you've been doing," I said.

She didn't say anything.

"We're going to go inside and find out what's been going on," I said. "Today is the day that everything comes out."

Silently, Shanna followed me into the bank. A hush fell over the clerks. The affair had been the subject of their gossip. Perhaps they'd seen Paul the banker pick up the call on a burner phone. Surely, they'd seen him hike up his pants in alarm and flee out the back door.

My anger came in waves. I summoned the president of the bank. "I want a statement from my business account right now."

The clerk behind the desk was frightened. Her eyes nervously shifted from me to the president. The president told her to do as I said.

I looked down at Shanna. She averted her gaze.

"Are there any accounts I don't know about?" I asked.

"Yes," Shanna said.

"Any safety deposit boxes?"

"Yes," she said, softly. "One."

Shanna and I held a joint account. I didn't have my own. I made one connection after another. The more it came together, the hotter my face felt.

"I want the safety deposit box opened now," I said. "I want the statements, too. From the minute the account was opened."

The president looked at Shanna. She nodded, her eyes downcast. She produced the key to her deposit box and handed it to the president.

"Come back at 5:00," the president told me. The customers would be gone by then.

DESTINED TO FAIL

Shanna and I got back in her SUV. I sat on the driver's side with the door open.

"Now we know that money is being smuggled," I said, calmly. "So, what else is going on?"

"Nothing," Shanna said.

"Well then," I said. "I guess we'll just sit here and wait for your boyfriend."

That was when she broke.

"Yeah," she said. "I've been having an affair."

We sat there in the car for a moment without speaking. As I attempted to process everything, the adulterer emerged from hiding. Paul approached the front doors of the bank.

"Hey, asshole!" I called.

Paul swiveled and froze when he saw me.

"Heard you had a little fun behind my back."

"I don't know what you're talking about."

I pointed to Shanna. "She told me everything."

Paul caught sight of her in the front seat. In spite of her pretty dress, she looked defeated and tired-eyed. Paul's face lost all color. He knew it was over.

"I treated you as a friend," I said. "And this is how you treat me?"

Paul stood there, a coward in a suit. I realized just how ugly he was. It was inconceivable to me that there could be an ounce of sex appeal or such a calculating mind in that flabby, disgusting carcass of a body.

I looked at Shanna. "I'll see you at home in ten minutes."

I knew where Paul lived. While he was still captive at work, I drove to his house. I rang the doorbell. Paul had three little girls, and one of them came to the door.

"Is your mom here?" I asked.

She called for her mom, and a second later, Paul's wife appeared, puzzled to see me. I pretended nothing was wrong.

"Could you come out to the truck? I need to tell you something."

She sat beside me on the passenger's seat.

"I've got bad news," I said, aware I was about to ruin her life. "I just busted your husband and my wife. They're having an affair."

"You're telling me…" she said slowly, "Paul and Shanna are having an affair?"

"Yes."

"How sure are you?"

"One hundred percent. I was just at the bank and confronted her. She admitted to it. They both did."

"You're lying."

"I wish I was."

Her eyes filled with tears. "This isn't his first time," she said. Paul's wife silently got out of the truck and walked back into the house, hiding devastation with her hands.

I pulled out of the drive. On my way home, I called Shelley.

DESTINED TO FAIL

"Come to the house," I said. Nobody had believed me about my wife, and I needed a witness. "Shanna's been screwing the banker."

Shelley was shocked and said she'd be right over.

"You have one minute to tell me everything."

Shanna told me that the affair had lasted a year and a half. She explained how she had illicitly withdrawn money from the Ace Dental business account.

"How much?" I asked.

She said she didn't know. She had a separate phone she used to call the banker, and a phantom email account, too. She told me where they had conducted their affair, which included both our house and Paul's.

Shanna told me about the masterplan they had devised between them. She had slipped the money from the account into the secret safety deposit box. She'd taken the money from the box and driven it, with our kids in the backseat, to northeast Iowa to her father's place. Her father had saved the money for her. Paul and Shanna figured, after enough time had passed and sufficient funds had been amassed through her embezzlement, they could make a life together with our kids and his three little girls.

"In order to raise them with the right religion," she said.

I put my head in my hands.

Shelley watched the whole thing in silence. Afterward, she looked at me. "I had no knowledge of any of this," she said. "And I would never condone it." Conflicted, Shelley drove home. I wondered whose side she would take.

After 5:00 p.m., the president's office was serene. The bank was nearly empty. Neat, carpeted silence hid any trace of the grief that had unfolded earlier.

I stood over the president as he opened the safety deposit box. All my grueling thirty-hour shifts, my anxiety, and my hopes were piled together in a meager hill of cash. It was only $1,000. The rest, an unquantifiable amount, was gone, irretrievable. Today had already been painful. Seeing a piece of my stolen earnings drove the wound deeper.

"You know, they were having an affair," I said. "My wife and your employee."

The president looked down at his Oxfords. "We all knew something was going on. Since she was a customer and a signer on the account, though, there was nothing illegal."

I knew the president of the bank was a decent man put in a difficult position. Still, I stewed in fury.

"If that piece of shit isn't fired immediately," I said, my eyebrows raised, "everyone in Omaha will find out *your* employee was having an affair *and* stealing money from one of your clients' accounts."

The president looked me in the eye. "He'll be fired the next morning." He was sincere.

Christmas mocked me from storefront windows as I drove back to the house.

DESTINED TO FAIL

BLUR

That night, I clutched myself. I had known all along my marriage was over, and still it wrecked me. This had been no innocuous fling: it was physical and emotional, with their futures projected. To cheat was one thing; to steal from our business was another.

When I'd come to the United States, the fear and isolation were debilitating. My father knew one type of cruelty, but at least it had its roots in his being well-meaning. This, in contrast, was heinous.

I demanded the login to the phantom email account, and Shanna gave it to me. After we put the kids to bed, I read everything, while she cried in the other room.

On the Monday of our anniversary, a week or so prior, Shanna and Paul had agreed to meet at his house. Afterward, Paul had written to her. He'd said that something had seemed off with her that day. Shanna had replied she'd felt guilty, because it was our anniversary. Paul had downplayed that. For him, this kind of thing was another day at the office.

I forwarded the emails to myself and printed them all. I had won, though in an empty way.

Later, I asked Shanna, "Why did you let it get this far? You grew up in a broken home. Why did you do this to your kids?"

She said nothing.

The next night, I tucked my kids into bed. My heart broke when I turned out their lights. Then, I closed the door to the guest bedroom and lay there, staring at the ceiling. The affair had marred our house. The pillows on the bed stank with defilement. So did every floorboard I had sanded, each threshold I had measured.

My children worried me the most. I wanted to stay with them at the house, to keep the normalcy alive. The idea that they lived and slept in that unclean place made me uneasy.

As the weeks went on, I resolved to get out. I began sleeping in the basement at work and saw my kids for dinner. I played with them and tucked them in. All they knew was that their daddy worked a lot. They forgave me when I was absent. They knew nothing, and Shanna and I kept it that way.

As the winter months wore on, more of my things came with me to the Ace Dental basement. March arrived, and I didn't fight with my wife over property or furniture. I just left.

DESTINED TO FAIL

"You wanted everything we built, but you didn't want me. Go ahead," I said, throwing my clothes in the backseat of the car. "You can have it *all*."

I felt worthless. I hated Shanna's guts. I cursed her and called her things far worse than *backstabber*. We didn't communicate anymore, save for when it concerned the kids.

Shanna had seen me work for hours on end. She'd seen me wander in, bleary-eyed, to sleep for two hours, only to go back to work for another thirty. If she had at least talked to me about being unhappy and wanting to be with someone else—someone unmarried, without three children—I would have been all right. I had known the marriage wasn't working for a while. Cheating in itself, I thought, was perfectly forgivable. I had messed up, too. But her betrayal was deeper than mine.

She sent me fifty emails out of desperation:

I'm sorry. Let's fix this. For the sake of the kids.

They gathered dust in my inbox.

My little children had always been human reminders to work harder. I'd weathered this cursed job, with its long hours, for the sake of my family's financial security.

I wrote a brief, sour reply:

You didn't think about them. Why the hell should I?

Shanna and I put the house on the market in the middle of the recession. Some part of me felt relieved the marriage was over. It had come in second to everything else. For seventeen years, I had been constantly sleep-deprived, which had made me short-tempered.

Another part of me wondered why Shanna stayed so long.

I lay at the bottom of a vortex. When my mom called, she heard the sadness in my voice. She knew about the separation but not the extent of the situation: the infidelity or my technical homelessness. I didn't speak a word of it to anyone. But her intuition sensed something was awry.

"I'm going to Spain for a month to visit my family," she said. "Why don't you come for a week? You'll take some time away from work and meet them."

I had never met the maternal side of my family. I had seen my mom's sweet handwritten correspondences from them and always wanted to visit. Now, I ached to flee.

But everything was in shambles, from my finances to my immigration status. My documents were not in order for me to leave the country: I had a Green Card, but my Jordanian passport was ancient and useless. Whatever I had to do, I resolved to cement my citizenship and get an American passport.

Tony called one day, in midwinter. "I've got something to tell you," he said.

DESTINED TO FAIL

"I need to tell you something, too," I said. I always told Tony everything and needed to just be out with it. We met for pizza.

"You start," Tony said.

I didn't know where to begin.

"Why don't you start?" I said, anxious.

"I'm gonna ask Jill to marry me," he announced.

An impassioned "she's the one" monologue became sotto voce as I blacked out in relief. I was elated for Tony and realized I had almost ruined his day.

"So, what did you have to tell me?" Tony asked.

I didn't have the heart to deflate him with the news. I made sure Tony didn't know about it until after his wedding that August. When I finally told him, he only knew that we had separated, nothing more. As he listened to the details of the infidelity and embezzlement, though, his mouth fell further open. For anyone who knew Shanna, the story was hard to believe.

As I riffled through the mail from the old house one day, and found a letter from Immigration and Naturalization. My naturalization application had been accepted. Shanna and I were summoned for an interview to go over the paperwork and finalize my citizenship.

I hadn't heard a whisper from them in ten years. *I got married to get this letter,* I thought. It was curious that it should arrive *now*.

A few weeks later, I stared at myself in the mirror. The morning sun illuminated the bags under my eyes. I fastened the first button on my suit and drove to the Immigration Office. A thought to tell Shanna briefly popped into my head. *Absolutely not*, declared my better judgement.

In the waiting room, an elegant woman emerged. She called Shanna's name and then mine. I stood up to follow her.

"Where's your wife?" she asked.

"She got *really* sick last night," I said, feigning concern. "I think she has mono. I couldn't figure out how to reschedule overnight."

The woman was horrified. "Oh! There is *no* need to reschedule!" she assured me. "Come with me. We'll finish your interview."

The woman asked a few benign questions and stamped some papers.

"Am I done?" I asked.

"Yes, you're done. I hope your wife feels better!" she said.

Fourteen years after I'd gotten married, a formal invitation came in the mail, and I was sworn in as a citizen on March 26, 2010. A judge spoke and three men dressed in stars and stripes sang, a singing flag. Fifty immigrants and I stood and said the Pledge of Allegiance. I didn't tell a soul I was there.

DESTINED TO FAIL

An envelope from Immigration and Naturalization arrived one morning a few weeks later. The crisp, navy booklet fell into my hands. My posture softened in relief.

As I worked late on the evening of October 7, 2010, my phone buzzed. My friend was on the other line. I knew his request was for a wingman.

My ringtone turned into a seven-minute soundtrack. On the fifteenth call, I picked up.

"Can't," I said. "Busy."

"Come on, man," said my friend. "Stacey brought another girl with her. I just need this favor."

"I've got stuff to do," I said. "What about your other friend, what's-his-face?"

"What's-his-face is busy. *Please?*"

"Fine," I said. My friend sent me an address. I knew this neighborhood; it was enveloped in an eerie silence any time I drove through it.

The friend called me again on the road. "Where are you?" he whined.

"I'm pulling up to your place," I said, leery of the dark street. When I parked in front of the house, the silhouette of a woman, the foreground in a yellow-window landscape, was the only subject on a deserted porch. A small light danced on her brow. I assumed it was the smoldering end of a cigarette.

"Is she the third wheel?" I sighed at him over the phone. "You know I can't stand smokers."

"Gimme some space with Stacey," said the friend. "Just talk to her."

I walked past the woman into the house, where my friend and his date lounged in the living room. I announced my presence, and my friend glared. The woman came in behind me, yet she didn't reek of cigarette smoke; the light must have come from her phone. She seemed exasperated but relieved at being free of the person on the other line.

I got along with Stacey's friend. She had piercing blue eyes and brown hair, and her name was Natasha. The four of us went dancing. Natasha and I talked all night. She was kind and witty. Our conversation carried over to the car, where we drove to a Village Inn. We sat in the dimly lit parking lot at 2 a.m., our conversation still dynamic. Even the silences buzzed.

In the early morning, I asked Natasha for her number. She tossed her hair back and smiled. "If you want my number that bad, get it from Stacey," she said.

I was gobsmacked, but it tickled me. As I got back in the car with my friend and Stacey, I sheepishly asked her for Natasha's number. She obliged.

Afterward, I went back to the lab and worked until sunrise. When I looked up, it was 8 a.m., and I decided to text her.

DESTINED TO FAIL

I crafted a message, and cautiously pressed *send*. The phone sang with the notification of her reply. My thumbs flew over the keyboard in response. Over the next day, we texted.

I had plans to go out with some friends that night and invited her along. We decided to go for a bite to eat beforehand. At the sushi restaurant, the wait for a table was two hours.

"How long is the wait for takeout?" I asked. They said twenty minutes.

At 10:30, Natasha and I drove a bag of takeout to the park. The moon was a bright egg in the night sky, and the temperature was mild. Parks closed at 10:00 in Omaha, but we trespassed anyway. We sat on the bed of the truck, talking and eating sushi. Inevitably, a pair of headlights pulled up, and a security guard squinted up at us. He was a pea-sized, scrawny fellow who you could tell was overcompensating by being the security guard at a park.

"Park's closed," he said. "You gotta get outta here."

I looked down at him and shooed him away. "We'll leave when we're finished eating."

He huffed and drove off. Not five minutes passed before three police cruisers pulled up next to the truck. He had called the cops on us.

"What's going on here?" one of them said.

"We're eating sushi," I said. "Want some?"

I promised the officer that we were responsible adults and would leave as soon as we'd finished eating.

Afterward, Natasha and I went downtown and met up with my friends. In the lights of bars and restaurants, we really saw each other.

During that period, I was going out and meeting lots of people, but my sadness had hindered connection. I really liked Natasha. No stress of commitment followed her. I resisted change, but she felt comfortable.

I was preoccupied with a suffering business, a stupid amount of work, and an imminent divorce. She met me in my worst state. I was frank with her.

"I just got out of a seventeen-year relationship." I told her all she needed to know.

I was initially reserved with Natasha. My last relationship had ended catastrophically, and I didn't want another. She understood, having come from a bad relationship, herself.

At this point, I needed to work on myself. To me, Shanna was a conspirator who had tainted my trust in people. But Natasha and I could talk for hours. The more time we spent together, the more I thought, *I can trust this woman.*

I needed time, and both of us had wounds that still smarted. Natasha needed time, too. It was a friendship at first, before we truly let each other in.

Natasha and me in one of our first pictures together, 2010

ANAS AFANA & STELLA BELLOW

MI FAMILIA ESPAÑOLA

My passport arrived at an opportune time. I flew to meet my mom in Tenerife in October 2010. I would've brought my children, too, but it was out of the question. Alone on an island far away in the Atlantic was what I needed now.

My mother's family had lived in the north of the island for eons. The formidable mountains reminded me of Jordan. Amman held secrets and history but existed for tourism. Jordan itself was beautiful because of the people. Tenerife, in addition to the emerald mountains and black beaches, was the same. In my mind, family was the link between Spanish and Arab culture. Kind, warm, and inviting, they wanted to have you at their table and feed you good things.

I was made to drink wine in Spain. I was sitting with my extended family when my cousin's husband asked me what I wanted to drink.

"*Agua, por favor,*" I said.

"*¡El agua es para el pato!*" the man roared: water is for the duck!

"What should I drink?" I laughed.

The Spaniard smiled, his arms spread wide as if to hug life itself. "¡Vino!"

In my time there, I wanted to get going and do things. But time on the island was a loose concept. My nervous jumpiness prompted my mom to put up her hand.

"Relax," she said. "You're on island time."

My mom in Tenerife, 1960s

Throughout my childhood, I had seen a black-and-white photograph of my parents. The year was 1964. The newlyweds sat together on a deck with two dormant cannons, my mother in a handsome pencil dress. My great uncle's house was visible, peeking through the trees a little ways behind them.

My mom and me on the cannon deck, 2010

"We have to go to the cannon deck," I said. My mom and I and her cousins, Lola and Carmen, took a trail that wound its way around the edge of the island. After an hour or so, we found our way to the spot. My mom and I squinted in the sun for the camera, forty-six years later. The old house was still there, nestled in the trees beyond us.

I sat on beaches of black, sparkling sand. My innate extroversion emerged when I got to kicking around a ball with some Europeans. Before we knew it, two teams were established. Greece, Denmark, Germany, and Spain were represented. We laughed as hard as we played. Soccer banished my American-born anxiety. I was unbound again, kicking up the sand and water with the soccer ball one of them brought. For thirty minutes, I relished the present. Adrenaline kicked in. Fear danced off my shoulders.

I went hiking with my Spanish family. I drank from a fountain that used to be the only source of water on the island. Legend was whoever drank from it would return to Tenerife. I climbed the rock and cupped my hands to drink and wash my face with the sweet, cold water.

My mom and I wanted to discover more about our ancestry. I knew a little. My DNA test was recent: I was mostly Middle Eastern, fourteen percent Italian, and twenty-six percent Spanish. My ancestors had emigrated from Italy to the Canary Islands in the 1800s. Perhaps this is why I loved my Italian friends. Or why my rage, when I flew into one, was a brilliant scarlet.

My mom located my great-aunt, our last living relative who knew my grandfather. We went to visit her as she neared her one-hundredth year. Her eyes gleamed beneath her wrinkles. I found all her photo albums stashed in a cupboard and unearthed photos I had never seen from my parents' wedding. Among my monochrome aunts and uncles, I discovered the photo of a stern man in his thirties, posing in a three-piece suit.

"Who's that?" I asked.

"That's your grandpa," said a relative. I gazed at the photo in amazement, and fragments of myself stared back. A familiar lock of curls rolled across my grandfather's forehead. My hair behaved the same way when I neglected to rake it with gel.

"He looks important," I said. "What did he do?"

"He worked in the jewelry business."

"I make jewelry, too," I said, incredulous.

To know I had an ancestor like me gave me solace.

Looking through the Spanish family photo album

My maternal grandfather, Ata Zatar

A few days before I left, forty to fifty members of my family gathered for a potluck in the park. They were all excited to meet me. They brought home-cooked dishes and laid them on the table with pride. We ate from a massive platter of steaming paella. It was a comfort to be with my relatives, who had loved me before we'd met.

When our last day in the Canary Islands came around, the pain returned. *I could just escape,* I thought. *I don't have to go back.* I imagined a world where I could stay in Tenerife.

My cousin Maria Teresa and I hiked a path in a remote part of the island. No one touched the earth but us. The sun set as we walked.

"Is everything all right with you, Anas?" she asked.

I had a far-away look in my eyes. "Yeah, I'm fine," I said, smiling. When I thought she wasn't looking, misery overtook my features. My eyes were downcast on the trail.

Her powers of observation were keen. "Are you sure?"

"Yeah, I promise." *If only she knew.*

We reached the precipice. The edgeless Atlantic spread out before me. The last rays of sunlight poured, brilliant, from a chasm in the clouds. Maria Teresa let me be. We sat in silence for a while as I gazed over the outstretched leg of the island, deep in troubled thought.

I watched the sun's last rays light up the water's surface. A breeze rustled the wild grass. I heard my cousin inhale the salt of the sea. To never return to Nebraska was tempting. But the faces of my children took form in my mind and interrupted all fantasies of escape. They, and no one else, were my reason to push forward. If I abandoned them, I could never forgive myself.

After forty-five minutes, Maria Teresa looked at me.

"Are you ready?"

I wasn't. "Yeah. Let's go."

DESTINED TO FAIL

I wanted to be forever in the sun. To hike the mountains, overlooking the expanse of the sea. With my family, the Spaniards, warm and kind beside me.

Teary-eyed, I said goodbye to my family. I was proud to be related to them. I wanted to stay, but so much was unresolved, and I would not let another incomplete life sail into the void. I felt dismal on the flight to mainland Spain.

The expansive airport in Madrid was abnormally empty. The commotion that usually bounced off the high ceilings had ceased. The Americans on our flight had arrived on the mainland without knowing that every major Spanish union was on strike. The bankers, the fishermen, the taxi drivers, and sanitation workers were all at home in solidarity. Our connection to Chicago that day had been canceled.

Everyone due for a flight back to the States was put up in a hotel. "We may have a flight to Chicago tomorrow night," the passengers were told. "Or we may not. We'll cover your hotel expenses tonight, but tomorrow, if you're all still here, you're on your own."

I had spent a hundred and ninety-four of my two hundred euros in Tenerife. My mind's eye saw my wallet sitting on my desk in Omaha. I couldn't even go on vacation without something going wrong. Still, I was excited to see part of Madrid.

I took a shuttle to the hotel and dropped my luggage. Plaza Mayor wasn't far. The Metro cost one euro. I mapped myself there, then walked through luminous cathedrals, past the soccer stadium, through markets, and down cobblestone streets. I talked to people in my mediocre Spanish and took pictures until my camera died.

    I wandered until well past sunset and into the late hours. Hearty, drunken laughter poured from open windows. I meandered back to the hotel at 3:00 in the morning and got a few hours of sleep. I promptly arrived in the lobby at 6:30 a.m., where the other passengers and I waited nervously for a shuttle to the airport. To our relief, one arrived.

    At the airport, the passengers were unbothered by security, who must have been on strike as well. We waited for three hours. The confusion compounded as we sat around. Finally, a couple of pilots sauntered up to the plane and fired her up. When we finally took off, there was widespread relief. Ten hours later, we landed in Chicago.

Omaha was overcast, the air crisp with harsh truths. The city seemed to shrink as I reestablished myself there. I realized it was a small town where lots of people knew me and my business. I told almost no one my life was in pieces. Not even my closest friends knew.

    Shanna and I waited for an opportune time to break the news to the kids. Six-year-old Danah sat on the counter. I blinked back tears and insisted Shanna tell them. She compared it to Nader and Danah's grandparents in Iowa,

DESTINED TO FAIL

who were divorced, too. Nader was nine. He understood what was happening, and it brought him to tears. Danah felt the instability but understood little. I felt saddest for them. I knew they would be forced to roll with the blows their parents dealt each other. They were small, and the foundation beneath them had ruptured.

We sold the house I'd built in April for $20,000 less than it could have gone for. We had to compensate for the economic crash. Shanna and the kids stayed there for some time then moved into a small apartment.

We accomplished the divorce process on our own. Shanna and I filed the paperwork and squared everything away. I practiced my speech all night before we were due in front of the judge. I wrote some notes on my hand. *This is a case,* I thought, *so naturally I'll have my say.*

That morning, I put on a suit and stood next to my ex-wife at the courthouse. The judge paid me no heed. He peered intently over his spectacles at Shanna.

"Are you here to finalize the divorce?" the judge asked her.

"Yes."

"Have you tried everything to salvage this marriage?"

"Yes."

"I'm giving you full custody of the kids."

I stared at the judge in shock. I would only see my kids Wednesday nights and every other weekend. Afterward, I read more about custody in Nebraska. Aside from some dire exceptions—drug addiction, alcoholism, or clinical insanity—mothers were almost automatically given custody.

Shanna pretended to read over the paperwork as we walked out of the courthouse. I glared at her, aggrieved.

"You've gotta be crazy, if you think I'm going to see my kids once or twice a week," I said.

"Don't worry," Shanna said with a sigh. "We'll figure something else out on our own."

I blasted Metallica in the car. I wanted to burn down the state of Nebraska.

After the split, Shanna turned selfish and unreliable. She absent-mindedly picked through boyfriends like a bowl of cherries. She frequently introduced the kids to strange people and didn't consider their feelings.

On one occasion, Shanna brought them to the house of a boyfriend who had a daughter Danah's age. The daughter pleaded with Danah to sleep over. I heard, through my daughter, how her mother had forced her to stay overnight at a strange, single man's house.

I called Shanna. Forced patience informed my every syllable. "I have some things to give you." We arranged to meet after work in the parking lot of a corporate department store. At 5:15, dusk was settling and the big lights swarmed with insects. Our cars were far from the entrance. The lot was deserted as I approached the passenger's side. I sat beside her, closed the door, and tore the key from the ignition. The car's interior muffled my screams.

"How *dare* you put my daughter in a position like that?" I said, the fear for my small child rising in my voice. It took all I had not to strangle her.

My ex-wife grew pale as she watched me combust. My all-powerful index finger waved inches from her nose. She cowered.

When my rant ended, I threw the keys at her. Shanna assumed I had finished and started her car. I walked back to mine. She turned out of the parking lot, and I chased her. When I pulled up next to her, I slid a finger across my neck. My rage was so intense, it could have impaired my vision. Shanna glanced over at me, petrified. Her knuckles were white on the steering wheel.

Beneath my anger dwelled watery sadness. My children were the only reason I had to go on. Half the time, I didn't know where they were. I was driven to madness for them. I was prepared to kill, to go to prison and scratch numerals into damp walls. Their absence exacerbated my worry.

A few years before, Shanna and I had signed a notarized statement to go into effect in the event of our deaths or in the case neither of us could care for the children. I had tucked it away in my safety deposit box. My mind went to dark, angry places, but the existence of that statement comforted me. If my ex-wife and I each met horrible ends, if I saw the inside of a prison cell, the kids would go to my sister.

They would lead a good life, I thought. *Under the benevolent eyes of the doctor.*

Shanna was still the company bookkeeper. I figured her embezzlement-induced guilt would prevent her from doing anything unethical again, but I searched for a new CPA. A friend recommended one, and I gladly took the referral's phone number.

The days had turned short and cold when Debbie, the accountant, walked into the Ace Dental office. I shook her hand. Instinct usually told me about people, and I liked her immediately.

She sat in the office and pulled up QuickBooks on her computer. I gave her a sticky-note with all the passwords, then disappeared to do some work in the other room. For a few hours, Debbie poured over QuickBooks. When she called me in, I found her worriedly staring into the computer. She inhaled sharply and looked up at me.

"I'm going to need more time. But I'm not going to lie," she said. "It doesn't look good."

Debbie returned a few days later and went through all our QuickBooks entries again. Every payable she came across was overdue, marked in red. Among the culprits were my parents' house, multiple maxed-out credit cards, and a long list of unpaid vendors. Even if I were faultless, everything was in my name. Shanna and I both lacked experience, but she had overseen the finances. I realized now that she had financially devastated me and, by extension, the kids.

"We're over $150,000 now," said Debbie. "But I'm not nearly done. If you wanted, you could file for bankruptcy."

Absolutely not, I declared to myself. I shook my head. "Bankruptcy is not an option."

"We're gonna have to pay it all back," she said, "if you want to avoid it."

"Are you sure you're willing to take this on?" I asked. "I may not be able to pay you."

Debbie nodded compassionately. "Absolutely. I'll help you get through this."

At that moment, I realized what a wonderful person sat in front of me. We made a pact to pay it all off.

Shanna drove the kids to Iowa that day. When I knew she'd been on the road for an hour, I called her.

"You are no longer the bookkeeper. You are not allowed access to my finances. You are no longer allowed in the lab."

Shanna made no argument. Boy, it felt good to fire her.

Debbie and I changed all the passwords. We made certain she was barred from every financial loophole she could worm her way into. I sat down with the phone numbers of the unpaid vendors. They had all labeled Ace as cash on delivery while Shanna had been in charge of the finances. I called one after another. The first was to W. E. Mowrey, the metals company Carlton worked for.

"I was wondering what happened," said the owner of the company. "You're usually so good about paying us on time."

I told them about Shanna. "Now that I'm in control of what's going on," I said. "I'm going to pay every dollar back."

"Carlton speaks so highly of you," said the owner. "And I know you're good for it. I'll take you off our COD list."

The other phone calls were the same. I called up Nowak Dental Supplies, whose owner was my friend, Brandi.

"Don't worry," she said to me. She knew my situation. "Order what you need."

My ten-year record had been exemplary, and my vendors knew I was reliable. They continued to send materials to Ace as Debbie and I started to chip away at the expenses. She continued to find open loans and, inch by inch, discovered the extent of the debt: more than $250,000. I told her not to give me a paycheck so long as the debt was present.

"I don't want to hear the numbers," I said to Debbie. "Don't make me sit for meetings just to hear bad news. You do your thing, I'll do mine."

I had been paying Shanna's rent in return for the job, for the sake of the kids. Yet whenever I visited the apartment, Nader cried. His mother yelled at him once a day, because he was nine and full of beans. He jumped on the furniture and ran around late at night. He didn't understand that this was a rental and he couldn't disturb the neighbors. At the same time, Nader knew more than the adults would tell him. His tears broke my heart.

Shanna and I had walked away with $30,000 in equity from the old place in the suburbs. "I'll hang onto this," I said, in regards to her smuggling.

We agreed to put it toward a small house for her and the kids. I put the property in Shanna's name and excluded my own, in an effort to detach myself from her as completely as possible. A part of me knew the decision was unwise. But in the likely event of my bankruptcy, I didn't want my kids to lose their home.

I was broke. By then, I'd sold everything: the truck, the house. Any unnecessary payments would further weigh me down. I ran around in a black '97 Civic that seven-year-old Danah affectionately called Black Betty. It was a car that nineteen-year-old me would've driven, with the same smell and feeling as the VW Rabbit. I daydreamed of the moment when Ace Dental would escape the red zone of debt and I could buy a nice car.

One day, I was particularly hopeless. I looked over at Debbie.

"When we're doing all right—I mean, absolutely, a hundred percent, no debt at all—I want you to say, 'Go buy a car.'"

I saw the kids a few nights a week. I was careful not to burden them with my worries. As a child, money was never an issue. It always blanketed my feet, even amid Sudanese unrest or my family's vulnerability to covert forces. I only imagined the insecurity any talk of my financial woes would instill. Surely, a sort of fear I did not want my kids to know. I wanted to be something like my father in this respect. A force of security. Protective. Brave.

There were times when I checked my account and found zero dollars, and my heart would stop for a second.

"There always needs to be money on that credit card," I said to Debbie. There were to be no scary financial episodes, no whispers of a credit card declined, while my kids watched.

I didn't receive a paycheck. I survived and fed and clothed my children off that piece of plastic.

DESTINED TO FAIL

EIGHTEEN YEARS LATER

As I first assimilated into the US and kickstarted my life, the ambassador's career was coming to a close. Things had shifted out of his favor at work, and the threat of the Gulf War gained on little Jordan.

In the years following my dad's retirement, my parents moved to Missouri (first my mom, then my dad a year later). They wanted to be close to their children and grandchildren. My sister needed an extra hand; she was studying for the board exam and wanted another eye on her kids.

My brother had moved to the States in 1984. After over twenty-five years here, he got a new job and moved his family to Dubai. My parents found themselves alone in Missouri. The family bought them a house in Omaha a year before my life blew up, and it was solely in my name. I insisted on keeping up with the payments, imagining how mortifying it would be if they lost the house due to my error. An unbearable thought.

I could have stayed with them. The house had three bedrooms. But I would rather be living in the basement at work or homeless than let my parents in on my failure: thirty-four, divorced, and nearly bankrupt.

Life tired and weakened me. It was a demon, this thing of being broke and indebted. Every day, money preoccupied my consciousness as more tabs and grievances arose. I struggled and worked, but it was futile. Perpetual.

Sometimes, a mantra stilled my worries: *as long as I'm breathing, everything's fine.* Inexplicably, this helped. I tried to inculcate myself with optimism as things fell apart.

I didn't have an official residence. The basement was an in-between place to eat and sleep. When the kids were with me for the night, I had to be inventive. Committed to being the fun parent, I bought them a tent and filled it with pillows and blankets.

"It's a camping trip!" I said, forcing a twinkle in my eye. The basement became a dark cave to Nader and Danah; the shadows of unused equipment were tall, looming trees by the glare of the flashlight. Roly-poly bugs were their small, humble friends from the dirt. Sometimes, Danah would walk up the stairs, a blanket in tow, because she got scared of the creepy basement. I made a fort for her upstairs, so she could sleep close to me. While Nader slept downstairs, I worked through the night.

In the morning, Danah would prepare me Cheerios and cheese blocks for breakfast at the lab. I called her lovebug because of how thoughtful she was. She would see my fingers, crooked from overworking, and pretend to fix them with Q-tips and a bottle of hand cream. In addition, she did my makeup and painted my nails.

Once she asked, "Daddy, can I draw on your pants?"

"Yeah," I said.

She picked up a purple Sharpie and drew flowers and butterflies on a pair of my jeans. When I put them on to go to the car parts store, the men in their Carhartts and cargo pants gave me looks of disdain. I didn't care. Danah was happy, and that was all that mattered.

Danah does my makeup

Me and the kids at the cabin

A friend had a one-bedroom cabin on the Elkhorn River that he rented to me for cheap. It made me relieved to be there, instead of spending all my time in the basement.

The kids played in the yard and drove around in a golf cart. I raised chickens. The kids loved the cabin. It was cool and contributed to an appearance of normalcy. My therapy was my children and the sound of the river.

Nader and Danah in the golf cart

I was working alone at the lab one Saturday, while the kids were with Shanna. The thought of them prompted a pang of paternal worry: *I haven't heard from them in too long.*

I called Nader, who had a cell phone, but he didn't pick up. I called Shanna, and the dial droned on forever. I tried Nader again. Once. Twice. Finally, my son's voice crackled in my ears.

"Hey, Dad."

Through the phone, I heard the sound of the interstate. "Where are you going?"

"Des Moines."

I pinched my temple. Shanna and I had made an agreement that the kids wouldn't go out of state without the other's knowledge.

"Why are you going to Des Moines?"

Nader didn't answer.

"Give the phone to your mom," I said. There was a few seconds of static.

"Hello?"

"Where are you going?"

"Des Moines."

"I thought we had an agreement," I said, exasperated. "Why are my kids going to Des Moines?"

"My boyfriend is from there. He's having a family reunion," she said.

I went ballistic and slammed the desk. Pens and tools clattered. The other line beeped and went silent. I called Nader again. No answer. Shanna had taken away his phone. I was sure of it.

I sat at my desk and stared into space. I got up and walked down to the basement. It was mostly storage: boxes strewn and stacked alongside some backup equipment, and my mattress in the corner under the pipes.

In a moment, the whole of me shook. I picked up a box and threw it across the room. I kicked a five-gallon bucket. A battle cry came from my ribs, and I punched the wall. I hurled what I could from one end of the room to the other, smashing things and yelling. I had never felt wrath like this, so blinding I could cry.

DESTINED TO FAIL

At the end, the basement looked like a town in the wake of a hurricane. As I stood in the center of the devastation, my ears strained for footsteps above me. I heard nothing.

I lay on my mattress that night, too upset to work. *This shit is over*, I seethed. Shanna had ultimate control of the kids. She could do whatever she wanted with them. Introduce them to strange men one after another, in-state or out. My music shuffled, and Metallica played. I wondered why I liked that band so much, with their troubled lyrics. James Hetfield must have been in a dark place, too.

I saw the pipes before I closed my eyes.

On Sunday, I awoke at 4:00 in the morning. My eyes panned from the ceiling to yesterday's explosion. I made coffee in the dark and rustled around for some trash bags. Instead of working, I cleaned. I swept and took out the trash and dusted off an Ace Dental plaque to hang over a gash I made in the wall. By Monday, the basement was spotless. An employee went downstairs to use the sandblaster and marveled over how clean it was. If only anyone knew.

When my children were little, Tony's parents watched over them. Tony's father and I shared an unwavering devotion to our families. *Benny is me*, I often thought. We had deep affinities for each other.

Benny with baby Nader

Benny, Lucy, Nader, and Danah, 2010

Benny had Alzheimer's in the last years of his life. He slowly succumbed. Tony and his family refused to put him in a home, and Lucia looked after him. In late May 2011, the hospice nurse said he might not make it through the night. A priest read Benny his last rites, and I sat in grief with Tony as the night wore on. Something heavy sat on my stomach, as if I, too, were losing a father. The house was full of bereft family members.

I didn't want to go. "I'm not leaving your side," I said to Tony. I slept on the floor.

Benny passed away in the morning. The family stood around their beloved patriarch until his last breath. Everyone in the house was heavy with sorrow. It hung in the living room air.

Tony called a few days later. "I want you to know," he said, "you're going to be a pallbearer." The family had made funeral arrangements. I was among the six men chosen to carry the coffin, our grief hidden in our stiff black suits.

I stood in the front line on the right side. Honor held me upright as I carried Tony's father to rest. Benny's death was another blow. Everything, everyone was leaving, dying.

At this point, my depression was debilitating. *I have to get away from here.* I daydreamed of escapes as I worked: Madrid or lush, mountainous Tenerife. With all my being, I longed for Jordan.

In August 2011, I announced to Rebecca and the others at the lab that I was going to Jordan for three weeks. My mother and children were coming with me. The employees were not happy. Ace was going down the drain, and I wanted to leave the country. Debbie was furious.

"Are you ridiculous? Do you *see* the amount of debt you're in? You're seriously going to make me come up with that out of thin air?"

The depression made me indifferent. "You guys hold down the fort," I said. "I just want to go home."

Shanna signed some paperwork and had it notarized, so I could take the kids out of the country. I booked two flights: Chicago to Paris, Paris to Amman. I had recently found a photo of my mom and me from when we lived in Paris. I was about nine in it, and I leaned against her. She wore a black dress, while I was zipped into a sky-blue jacket. We stood, unsmiling, in front of the Eiffel Tower, vertical against an overcast French sky. Perhaps seeing the photo for the first time in years manipulated my memory, but I remembered it being windy.

DESTINED TO FAIL

Mom and me in Paris, 1980s

My mom, my kids, and I arrived in Paris some decades later. The sun shone as we walked among the tourists. My kids stood for a picture with their grandmother. I smiled as they leaned against me in the same way.

"When your kids are ten," I told them, "come back to Paris, and take the same picture."

"Oh yes, we will," my kids said, cheerily. The tradition was in safe hands.

Me and the kids at the Eiffel Tower, 2011

I boarded the next plane with my children and instructed them to buckle their seatbelts. I felt they were safer with me, and I was glad to have them for three weeks at least. As the plane took off, my mom opened a book to the page she'd marked, and people chewed gum and opened their laptops. My mind raced.

DESTINED TO FAIL

Soon, the country I had left long ago materialized, and Amman greeted me from below. I had wanted to come home so fervently. *But not like this.* Not as I was now. I felt like a failure in every way.

I walked through the international airport in Amman. The pain from June 1993 hung in the air. I stood in the same place where, at age seventeen, I had hugged my mother goodbye. Early nineties déjà-vu rushed back, stinging and sad. Another eighteen years had passed since I'd been home.

My children walked in front of me to where Cousin Razi and my sister waited to greet us. I was elated to see them both. I didn't tell anybody else I was there.

We emerged from the fluorescent lights into the blazing August sun. A brilliant-blue sky greeted me. I inhaled, and my shoulders relaxed. I had escaped my Nebraskan existence.

In three weeks, I squeezed in all of Jordan. The kids and I traveled everywhere. For four days, we went to Aqaba, the only city on Jordan's little coast. Nader liked to snorkel, slapping on his mask and goggles before he ventured into the water. Danah loved to collect rocks. I searched around beside me, coming up with brilliant orange stones.

She ran back and forth, bestowing me with handfuls. "What do you think of *these*, Daddy?" Danah and I basked in the salt for hours.

A party of my relatives hiked Petra in the blazing heat. My kids, my mom, and a few nieces trekked through the Siq. Its cavernous red walls of sublime rock and stagnant waves of mountain towered over us. For a few miles, we walked along the path marked by footprints and grand caravans. Great undulating rock enveloped us in orange and amber.

We emerged from the warm halls of stone into a clearing. The family gazed up into the searing light at Al-Khazneh. We marveled at the sublime columns and ornaments in the bed of massive rock, which still stood upright a millennia after it had been carved by an ancient people. Everyone took pictures to remember they had seen the hand-chiseled monument for themselves.

Sweat poured from our brows, and our feet ached. The consensus among the women was to turn around. They yearned for an air-conditioned room and the swimming pool.

DESTINED TO FAIL

Nader and Danah at Petra

"Dad," Nader said, "I don't care about the heat. I want to climb."

"Listen," I said. "You lead. When you're done, I'm done."

I had told my children about a magical place called Petra. Nader wanted to see it for himself. For four hours, we climbed the sandstone and explored the ancient ruins and caves of swirling sediment. In another life, I had been a boy and climbed there, too. I swelled with pride. My son scaled the rocks with absent-minded joy.

Nader and Danah saw Jordanian relatives they had never met before. Their cousins were loving and kind, making the kids from Nebraska feel like one of them. I knew Jordan was always about the people. Nader was struck by it.

"I've just met them," he said. "They act like they've known me forever."

"You are family," I said. "You're my kid. That's how it is here."

Losing everything back home was a possibility, but I let my family remain in the dark. I smiled till my face ached. They knew about the divorce, but I didn't mention anything else. "My life is *fantastic*," I declared, and they all believed me. Shame pooled at my center.

I wished three weeks could be a month and even entertained the thought of staying. *I'll send my mom and the kids home and hide out in the desert.*

I pushed the fantasy aside and donned my war paint. *I'm going back. I'll save everything or die trying.* I threw my arms around Cousin Razi and said goodbye to my sister. I assumed my father's stoic calm.

Me and Razi

On the plane, I sat next to my children. My throat threatened to close. *You will not cry*, I thought on a loop. The sound of the engine wailed. The plane rushed forward, then soared over the country I loved.

I looked over at the kids. They were both crying. They missed Jordan, too.

"We can't tell the pilot to make a U-turn," I joked.

My tears still gathered at the sight of them. I lost all composure and cried, almost as unrestrained as my children. I wiped a tear away with the palm of my hand and watched the golden-brown of the city grow faint below.

Back in Omaha, Debbie was livid about the expenses I had accumulated. My travels around Jordan and the visit to Paris had racked up our debt even further. I worked tirelessly over the next few months.

I was glad to see Rebecca, my work-wife. She had been with me since 2000, and we had weathered the business together. She was the anchor ceramist. An affectionate pillar to me, too, as life went downhill.

One or two people at Ace ticked me off. An employee named Kay stirred up unnecessary drama. My life was already too dramatic for my liking. I wanted to work in peace and made plans to fire her. December neared, and she handed me a slip of paper.

"I'm giving my two-weeks' notice," she said.

"Okay," I said. *Oh good, I don't have to fire her.*

I walked into Rebecca's office for a hello and some light gossip.

"You know, Kay just gave her two-weeks' notice," I said.

The color drained from Rebecca's face.

"Is something wrong?" I asked. "Are you sick?"

"She's not the only one," she said, quietly.

I thought she was joking. "What? Who's leaving?"

"I'm quitting, too," she croaked. She had received a job at another lab and couldn't endure the instability of Ace or its owner any longer.

DESTINED TO FAIL

I put a hand over my heart. My wife had left me. Now my work-wife was leaving, too. I sat at the desk, head in my hands. *I want to end this whole thing. I want it to be over.*

When Rebecca left, she took several accounts with her. The demands of work weighed more, and the hours grew longer. As it continued to hurl itself at me full-speed, I barely stayed afloat. The income was insufficient, under seventy percent of what the business needed to operate. I scrambled with two remaining employees. I covered three peoples' jobs.

People continued to leave, and their absence haunted the quiet. The silence became a dimension of its own, filled with otherworldly things. I heard the noises again; they became routine. When I lay on the mattress in the basement, the floorboards above me creaked. Even if he wasn't flesh and blood, the ghost named Harvey was still another soul there. His presence, even his pranks, were comforting.

The vacuum would start up, and I'd get up from my bench. "Very funny, Harvey," I'd say, as I flipped the switch to turn it off.

I hated being alone—sometimes it made me angry. The sounds of the floorboards would reassure me: *Harvey's here.* I talked to Harvey in the silence. "Thank you for listening to me," I said to him often.

Freddy called me one night.

"How are you?" he asked.

"Becca left," I sighed. "So, not so good."

"Sorry, man," Freddy said. "My guy Ned's leaving, too."

The conversation evolved, and it was a perfect puzzle. The jobs Ned usually covered for Freddy were the same ones I worked. Freddy worked in ceramics, like Rebecca.

"Until we figure things out," I suggested, "would you like it if I drove up to Des Moines a couple days a week? You could cover Becca's end, and I could cover Ned's."

We made a deal. Sunday night at 8:00, I drove two hours to Freddy in Des Moines. On Tuesday night at 10:00, I headed back to Omaha. Metallica played in the car, and it reflected the sadness I had to stuff down at work. The remainder of the week, I was in Nebraska, and I barely stopped to sleep, not to mention shower.

One morning in December, my eyes opened to the basement ceiling. I heaved a sigh at the brown pipes and beige walls.

I slept below Ace Dental when I was in Omaha, on a blow-up mattress. Roly-poly bugs burrowed through cracks in the floor. In the next room over, I showered standing on uneven concrete. It was a humble thing I'd built myself. Copper pipes. A bucket.

My things were all over and stuffed in a closet. I had never conceived of myself being here, of this as reality. It took on such unimaginable shapes.

DESTINED TO FAIL

ROCK BOTTOM

I wanted full custody of the kids. I needed to have them under my own supervision, to know where they were. Full custody was also a way out of paying child support. The monthly payments Shanna received—a little over $1,000—weren't going toward my children. I covered all their expenses on my own, as well as my parents' property, and Shanna's mortgage.

In my deliberations, I consulted a friend, a father who had gone through a divorce. He had been through the same custody fight I would soon enter. As was custom, especially in Nebraska, the mother had won the case.

"You don't have a chance at all," said the father. "You might as well save your money and your grief."

I was discouraged. Still, I asked around for the best lawyer for dads and received a name. They called him the Great White Shark, and I hired him right away.

The six-foot-four, broad-shouldered divorce lawyer came to greet me in the lobby of his practice. I followed him into the office, gleefully imagining the scene in court. He would merely stare into my ex-wife's soul, and it would be all he had to do. Shanna would faint on the spot.

"Well, is she an addict?" the lawyer asked. "Is she an alcoholic?"

I explained everything: all that Shanna had done to confirm my distrust in her. Her financial recklessness, and how she towed her children around to strange men's houses, sometimes out of state.

"I don't want to pay child support. She doesn't deserve it, and she doesn't use a cent of what I pay her for the kids," I said, knowing those weren't grounds for custody.

"You have an ice cube's chance in hell," said the shark.

"My kids are worth the gamble," I said. "I want to proceed."

As soon as I left the lawyer's office, the bills began to hit me. They were hefty and came in groups. Envelopes arrived with requests, letters, and forms from Shanna's lawyer. I didn't know what half of it meant.

In a way, the lawyers were a waste of money, just legal mercenaries who sent us monstrous bills. That was all they were good for. I had a strategy: I'd waste the money I didn't have to outlast Shanna. If she and I fought long enough, one of us would cave. My job was to endure. I cooperated with the lawyer's demands and dug further into the debt drain.

During Labor Day weekend, I parked Betty in front of Ace overnight. When Natasha dropped me off for work the next day, Black Betty was gone. My mind raced. The car had been stolen, I deduced. I called the cops, who screeched up in their cruisers.

"My car's been stolen," I said.

"Somebody rammed it into an ATM," they said. "It's been totaled."

The police credit union ATM was a block away from Ace. The thieves had hatched an epic strategy to rob the ATM: find and steal some vacant automobile, and bullishly plow into the cash machine. They had revved the car from a few yards away and rammed it into the ATM over and over until they put an enormous gash in the radiator. The engine bay burst into flames. The individuals had fled the scene. The cops had figured it was me who'd done it, until they watched the footage from my security camera that had caught the offenders at 4:00 in the morning.

I only had liability coverage on the Civic, and it was a total loss. While Natasha helped me get to work, I searched for another car. The next one I found was a silver Civic from the same year, one that Danah christened Silver Betty. After a few months, Silver Betty's transmission coughed and died out. My bad luck multiplied into another thing that bit the dust. I needed to come up with more money for it, almost $2,000.

I can't catch a break.

On a gray day in 2012, I awoke on the basement mattress. My phone rang.

"Hello?" I stared up at the pipes.

A dentist spoke on the other line. He introduced himself as Brian.

"We're struggling to find a lab," said Brian. "And I've seen your work. It's really good."

I lit up. "That's great."

"We've got three other doctors here, too, and they're definitely interested," Brian said. "Come down and see us tomorrow, will you?"

"Sure thing," I said.

Brian began using Ace Dental. The other doctors took an interest in my work, too. Soon, I worked for the whole office. *This is a start.* It was auspicious, the first hand offered to pull me from the drain. Stability twinkled from afar.

I mulled over thoughts of business on the drive to my parents' house one day soon after. I pulled into their driveway and opened the door, expecting to see my mom. But my father stood in the kitchen, alone. My mom wasn't there.

"Where's Mom?" I asked, lingering at the threshold.

"Come in," my dad said. "I want to talk to you."

I didn't like being alone with him. Unease abounded without my mom's presence. I always found some excuse to leave.

"No," I said, warily. "I think I'm gonna go."

"Come in," my dad repeated.

DESTINED TO FAIL

Against my better judgement, I walked into the kitchen. He began to lay into me.

"Why are you so dry with me? So business-like? You don't respect me, do you? You never show me affection."

My dad's ridicule was citrus on an open wound. Neon, searing pain overwhelmed the space behind my eyes. The wind rustled my shirtsleeves again.

I was back in Iowa, where the land, mysterious then, rolled on forever. At seventeen, I had squinted into the August sun as I watched my dad walk away. My brother-in-law had turned the key in the ignition, and the Oldsmobile drove off, growing ever smaller. The car had made the final right turn out of the lot, and disappeared.

I imagined my dad shouting, "Turn around!" and my brother-in-law whipping a U-turn. *Dad's gonna have some remorse,* I'd thought. *They're gonna turn around.*

For hours, it had seemed, I stood there. I'd searched the horizon for the car. But there was no sign of the Oldsmobile. They weren't coming back.

I had felt a profound loneliness, waiting there in vain. My adolescent mind had worked so hard to comprehend what had just happened. Gray hairs could have sprouted from my head in that moment. I didn't feel seventeen anymore.

The terror in my stomach had twisted into an unadulterated fury. For twenty years and more, it had gone unexpressed. Now, at age thirty-eight, I shook with rage.

"*You threw me in here!*" I bellowed. "*You* brought me here. You never *loved* me. You never supported me. I *resent* you. I have resented you so deeply for so many years, because I always had to do what *you* wanted. You never showed me I *mattered*."

My father denied it. "That's not true. I love you."

I was affronted. *That's not how things played out.* Every waking moment directly contradicted this. To suggest my life abounded with endless paternal love was nothing short of mockery. My mouth contorted in bitterness.

"You have never said that to me before in your life."

We fought. Rage spewed from our mouths. Somewhere in the middle of our argument, it reached a boiling point. The kitchen cabinets rattled. The house reverberated with our screams.

I stormed out. On the drive home, my knuckles gripped the steering wheel. The engine moaned as I exacted my fury upon the gas pedal. My breathing had begun to slow when my mom called.

"What did you do?" she asked, exasperated.

"I told him the truth. He wanted to hear it."

I should've left, I thought. *I can't be alone with him.*

My dad and I didn't speak to each other after that. This upset the family; they attempted multiple times to fix things between us. But I didn't want to mend bonds, not now.

DESTINED TO FAIL

I almost welcomed the distance. It bought me time to untangle myself. I was too weak of heart to face my father. I still felt like a failure.

I remembered a story Natasha told me of a bracelet that belonged to her grandmother. It was silver, with an ornate pattern, the kind you find on the ends of spoons. On a trip home to the East Coast, her grandmother had found an identical one and given it to Natasha's mother. It was an heirloom of the women in her family.

Natasha and I had broken up a few months ago. It was not as much of a breakup as time spent apart. After the fight with my dad, the pressure of work made time for a girlfriend impossible. I told her this. Natasha was sad, but she was good about it. She said she understood. Her absence was a void. I thought about her all the time.

Late in the evening on my birthday, when I'd hammered out all the work I could, I made an exact cast of the heirloom. *Only she will love this,* I thought. Her birthday was the day after mine. I held onto it with the intention of seeing her again. Something inside me, though I wasn't sure how or when, told me I would.

People fell out of my life for no good reason. At least, I knew the explosion with my dad was necessary. Pent-up resentment had plugged my insides since the day in the parking lot. The surplus of anger and the scarcity of hope had made me feel small. Wherever I could, I sought answers.

A progression of cold rains marked the early spring. In April, an unexpected balminess rose up from the Missouri River. A reminder of summer hung in the cornfields.

The clock struck two in the morning. I had been working on a tall stack of cases due in six hours. I stood up and stretched my legs. The work would keep me until 5:00 or 6:00 a.m., at least. Massive quantities of caffeine were necessary to propel me onward.

I propped the backdoor open and fired up the Nespresso. The night was clear and cloudless. I stepped outside to the fenced-in yard behind Ace and sat on a chair with my cup. I gazed upward. The formidable sky over the heartland dwarfed me. Her billions of eyes met mine.

Everything in the last four years had combusted. The marriage, the business, my home. Family eluded me. I had no idea where my children were. My father and I weren't speaking. I missed Natasha and didn't confide in my friends because I didn't want to burden them. I worked myself blind, and nothing good would come of it.

What if there's no way out. I knew nothing of the numbers. Hundreds of thousands in debt still hung over me and condemned me to fret and scramble, to live in isolated squalor in the basement. I breathed, but nothing filled me.

DESTINED TO FAIL

I was raised with God as an absolute. We were held in a culture and a faith that never questioned, only trusted. But my whole being was in anguish. I felt myself coming undone. Perhaps it was from mere exhaustion; tears rolled from my eyes, hot and unsuppressed. The sky listened as I spread my arms.

"Come on," I pleaded. "How much more are you going to throw at me?"

PART THREE
BECOMING THE PIRATE: 2014-2019

ANAS AFANA & STELLA BELLOW

STAN DARLING

I was friends with a doctor who was well-off and owned a condo. He wanted to sell it. The idea of any secure thing was tempting. The debt and the bad credit were my hindrances.

"I'll do anything to make sure I'm stable and my kids are stable," I told him. "But my credit score is garbage. My name is on every open loan. It's all over the debt. Nobody's going to give me any money."

Doctor Khan called his friend, Stan, who worked at a local bank in Fremont, Nebraska.

"I've got a good friend," Doctor Khan told Stan. "He's down on his luck. I can personally guarantee he won't screw you over on a loan."

With the good word of the doctor and a folder of paperwork from Debbie, I drove west to Fremont. I walked through the doors of Pinnacle Bank.

"Is Stan here?" I asked a clerk.

"He's expecting you," she said.

A man with a kind face came out to shake my hand. I followed him into his office. Stan cleared the mountains of paperwork off his desk. My eyes darted about the room. A pile of Stan's business cards faced me. *Vice President, Pinnacle Bank.*

Vice President? Gulp.

"So, Anas," Stan said, sighing as he sat down. "Tell me your story. When would you say you were at your best financially?"

I thought for a second. "2008."

"Start at 2008. Tell me the whole story. Until you sat down in front of me today," he said.

I told Stan everything.

"I had no knowledge of anything, of any finances. I only worked. My ex handled that stuff."

I gave Stan the folder, and he leafed through it. His spectacles reflected the screen of the computer. The bank hummed quietly with printers. Stan's mouse clicked.

"What are my chances for a loan?" I asked, filling the silence. I already knew the answer and didn't want to get my hopes up.

"Your credit is pretty awful," said Stan.

I knew he would say that. "Everything is in my name. I know. I just want to be able to provide a home for my kids," I said.

Stan looked up from the screen. "Oh, I'm going to give you the loan," he said.

I kept from gasping aloud. "What about the bad credit? The underwriters and everything?"

"I'm going to bypass them," said Stan.

"Thank you," I said.

We shook hands, and I walked into the parking lot. I threw the folder of numbers on the passenger's seat, rested my brow on the wheel, and cried in the muffled safety of my car. There were only so many times I could play "camping" with my kids in the basement. Or look after them at a rental cabin. I didn't have to perform anymore. Finally, we would have some semblance of security.

I spoke with Doctor Khan sometime after and thanked him profusely.

"I knew he'd give you the loan," he said. He dropped a key into my palm. "Here. Live there till you figure it out."

The key to the new home in my hands, I called Shanna and told her I needed the kids for an hour. I picked them up from school and drove them straight there. The condo had two bedrooms and an unfinished basement. I had been there before, to look around before the meeting with Stan. It was small but tasteful and modern. I had figured it was out of my price range. Now, my kids and I saw the place anew. We envisioned everything it would become.

"Dad, can I have a room in the basement?" Nader pleaded.

"Absolutely," I said. I was excited that Nader could have a room of his own.

Until the basement was finished, Nader used the master bedroom. I slept in the living room. My friends from soccer were construction workers and drywall contractors. They helped me, and were generous.

"Give us what you can," they said when they'd finished the downstairs. They trusted me, and I paid them in installments when there was money to spare. Nader made his own cove down in the basement. Danah made hers upstairs.

Tony and Carlo helped me move in, as they always did. My workstation was set up at home, so I could be there while the kids slept. I seldom slept in my own bed. Instead, I hunched over my desk until 3:00 or 4:00 in the morning and slept on the living room floor until 6:00. As the late nights accumulated, a divot formed in the carpet where I crashed. If my back was on a hard surface, there would be no temptation to hit the snooze.

In the mornings, I sprang up, determined, and brewed coffee. I made sure Nader and Danah had all their things before they got in the car. School was a thirty-minute drive from the house. My kids were never late to homeroom.

The relief of a new place meant that I could call Natasha. I held the sterling heirloom I'd made for her as we talked over the phone. We agreed to meet. "I'll come by your apartment," I said.

The bracelet I made for Natasha

When I gave Natasha the bracelet, she examined it in disbelief. She knew I inscribed all the jewelry I made with my Arabic signature. She found it under the ornate surface, next to the date.

"You made this five months ago," she said.

"Yes," I said. "I didn't know how, but I knew I would hand it to you in person when I saw you again."

I covered up any hint of a girlfriend to protect my kids. Natasha texted me one night and asked if she could stop by. *Sure*, I said. It was a school night, and the kids were asleep by then.

She arrived at the house around midnight. We sat at the kitchen table and talked about our days.

We heard a noise and then twelve-year-old Nader padded into the kitchen in a pair of gym shorts. He'd had trouble sleeping. His inquisitive expression demanded an explanation.

I introduced him to Natasha. We sat around the table for a while and talked, before Nader went back to bed. The next morning, Nader drilled me with questions while he put on his shoes before school. The strange woman sitting by his dad knew everything about him, and he knew nothing about her.

Danah quickly found out. She asked a million questions, too. I introduced Natasha to both of them in the following days. Once the kids met her, she became a more frequent benevolent presence. She and I painted their rooms in the condo whatever colors they wanted. Natasha was an interior designer, and she worked her magic to make the place feel like home. With her back in my life and a comfortable place to live, I started to feel good about myself.

Now and then, Debbie started to slip me a paycheck. This was rare; the debt was ever-present. I plowed through my days, wishing they were over as soon as I arrived at the lab. I was tired and needed a vacation.

Natasha and I decided to take the kids on a trip to the Dominican Republic. Natasha wanted to go somewhere, too—she'd traveled a lot as a kid and hadn't for some time. We wanted to go somewhere together and bring the kids. In July 2013, we put a little money together. The four of us drove up from Omaha and spent the day in Chicago, then flew out of O'Hare Airport to Punta Cana. On the beach, we covered ourselves with sand and smiled for pictures underwater. The kids bonded with Natasha. We loved Punta Cana and swore we'd return.

One evening, I was working at home when my phone buzzed. A name popped up on the screen that I hadn't seen in years: *Shelley*. She was Shanna's best friend and my friend, too, before the divorce. I had tried to gauge where her loyalty lied, but it was clear she had picked Shanna in the end.

I could hear Shelley breathing on the other line.

"Did you butt-dial me?"

"I didn't think you were going to answer," said Shelley. "Can I come over? I need to tell you something in person."

I said yes, but I didn't know what to expect when she sat down in front of me an hour later.

Shelley didn't say anything at first. She just looked at me. I had a hunch Shanna had given her the same royal treatment.

"The last time I saw you," I said, "my wife had just stabbed me in the back. Did she do something like that to you, too?"

Shelley nodded. "I'm sorry. I believed her over you. Shanna screwed me over."

"Why did you want to talk to me?" I asked.

"After what Shanna did to me, I realized I chose the wrong friend, and I wanted to correct that mistake. Shanna also told me some things about you that I know are wrong. She told me you were abusive."

Shelley showed me the emails Shanna had written to her mother, with Shelley carbon copied. They were from the last year of our marriage.

In one of the emails from early in the year, Shanna described an incident I was familiar with. On the way out the door to work, Nader had asked me if he could do something, and I'd refused. Nader had said, "Okay." In Shanna's account, though, I had screamed awful things at him and made him cry. Nader rarely got yelled at; he was such a good little boy.

The emails were all like this: distorted encounters that characterized me as verbally and sometimes physically abusive toward Shanna and the kids.

I was short with everyone in those days. Sleep-deprivation made every encounter draining. Perhaps this made it easy for Shanna to tell people her husband was something he wasn't. And, perhaps in some way, to justify the affair to herself.

I looked at Shelley, horrified.

"That's why I picked her side," Shelley said. "I thought she was the victim."

Another email was from a time in April that I also remembered. I had walked in and found Shanna drunk. I recounted the episode to Shelley, who told me she had gone to lunch that day with Shanna and Paul, the banker. Shelley had sat down to lunch with Shanna when Paul appeared.

"Paul's here!" Shanna had declared, feigning surprise. Then Paul had joined them. Shelley told me he would appear frequently at their lunches. Of course, Shanna had texted him where they were, but they pretended his appearance was a coincidence.

On that day in April, they'd all gotten day-drunk on Jägermeister. The three of them had been on an email chain afterward.

"That was so much fun," Shanna had written. *"Who cares that someone's husband got pissed."* That email was from the morning in 2009 when I had shouted at her.

It was also a written admission. I could have shown it to my lawyer. But I already felt bad about asking Shelley to witness my marriage explode and didn't want to get her involved more than she had been.

In the midst of the custody battle, the emails and false allegations made me angrier. I remembered going to a parent-teacher conference the year the marriage ended. It was with one of Nader's teachers, with whom I was usually on good terms.

Shanna and I were side-by-side when I asked her a question. When she answered, she only spoke to Shanna. The teacher wouldn't look me in the eye. That night, Shelley realized Shanna had used her as a smokescreen. Shelley was my friend again.

One of the people who witnessed my low point was my friend, Leo, an immigrant from Sicily. He was the head chef and owner of an acclaimed Italian restaurant in Omaha. He was always someone I could talk to, as I was for him—one tired immigrant to another.

"Anything you need," Leo said to console me. "I'm here."

"Thanks, Leo. I'm working on rebuilding things."

"You know, Anas, I could loan or even give you money," he said. "But I know you wouldn't accept it."

Leo was right: I would never take a handout. But Leo was down a chef at the restaurant, and I had a thought. "I know how you can help me," I said. "You could let me work for you."

Leo obliged and was glad for the help. I worked for him three days a week as a cook. The fundamental operation of the kitchen was familiar to me, from long ago in Iowa. I ran the grill and quickly learned Leo's way of cooking chicken, steak, and fish to perfection, for a table of two or a party of thirty. Wednesdays, Fridays, and Saturdays in particular were jammed and frenzied. At 5:00 in the evening, I drove from the lab to the restaurant and cooked until nine. Afterward, I was back at Ace until 2:00 or 3:00 the morning. The restaurant paid well. The work brought a little more in.

DESTINED TO FAIL

On my nights off from the restaurant, I stayed at the lab as late as my eyes would allow. Saturday nights crept into the wee hours. Sunday nights I was on the interstate to Freddy in Des Moines. Sleep was secondary. I ran to and fro to put the down-payment on the house and to pay for the basement and the expenses that followed.

As we tried to vanquish the debt, I was not on the payroll and stayed off it for the time being. I brought in as much money as possible, and bankruptcy was never an option. Things were so frenetic, I didn't have time to fear it, anyway.

Natasha radiated goodness. I had found her at my lowest. She knew every little thing about me, including the stuff I didn't tell anybody. I had never met anyone in the States who looked at the world the way she did. I had been thrust into darkness. Where I only saw a life that lacked, she saw an abundance.

"Everything's gonna turn out great," she said. She repeated the sentiment when I needed to hear it. Natasha and I were both broke, but it barely mattered—we made each other happy.

Later that year, she got a call.

"I got a job in Denver," she told me after. "What do you think we should do?"

There was a little back and forth between us.

"Work comes first," I said. "I think you should take it."

Natasha and I decided to stay in touch and stay exclusive. We were determined to see our relationship work, however long the miles stretched between us. I helped her move with the knowledge that I would see her again. We loaded the U-Haul and drove her to Denver. I spent the weekend and then flew back to Omaha.

Every day, one of us called the other. I flew to Denver. Natasha flew to Omaha. Or we met halfway, in North Platte, Nebraska, a small, quaint town almost parallel with the upper right-hand corner of Colorado. Goodbyes took place in airports swarming with travelers.

Our relationship was unique and strong in that it functioned when we were apart. But I missed her. Each time I drove back to Omaha, I ached, feeling devoid of her. The feeling spanned the weeks I didn't see Natasha and multiplied the more we were apart. I always wanted to know her.

On one spring day, Natasha and I met up in North Platte. We discussed realities. How hard and wretched the long-distance was. We talked about the big questions we had never broached before—what our futures held, and what we individually wanted.

I got back in the car and thought, *I want to marry this woman.*

On the drive back to Omaha, I envisioned a cliff where I'd stood on a visit to my cousin in California. My breath nearly left me there. I felt the salt of the Pacific and the wind on my eyelids. Shrubs and wild things grew at my feet.

Ooh, I thought. *That's where I'll do it.*

Back home, I called my cousin, Ziad.

"Hey," I said, "remember that cliff? We went there after we played soccer when I visited last time."

"Yeah," Ziad said. "Palos Verdes. What about it?"

"I'm gonna ask Natasha to marry me," I said. "And I want to do it there."

Ziad was thrilled. He was a drummer for a Pearl Jam cover band called Vitalogy, in addition to his main job as a software engineer. "You should come watch me play at the Whiskey a Go Go," Ziad said. "I'm doing a show on New Year's Eve." I obliged. I announced to Natasha that we were going to Los Angeles for New Year's to see Ziad on the drums. This was the diversion. Natasha was excited.

November of that year was bone-chilling. I went to pick up my kids from school one day in twenty-something-degree temperatures. When they came to the car, Danah was adequately bundled up, but Nader was in a spring jacket, and his teeth were chattering.

"Where's your winter coat?" I asked.

"I asked Mom. She said she doesn't have enough money," he said. "She told me to go talk to you."

I took my kids to the store and bought them top-of-the-line winter jackets. Then, I said to Debbie, "Don't pay this month's child support."

She was hesitant, but she saw my anger. If Shanna wasn't going to take care of the kids and buy them winter coats with my money, I wasn't going to give it to her.

Two weeks later, I got a call from a child-support enforcement agent. Shanna had turned me in. "You're being held in contempt for failure to pay child support," the woman threatened. "If you don't pay, you're looking at multiple fines and possible jail time."

Jail rang in my ears. I signed the check, and Debbie paid it immediately.

On a dreary February day in 2014, Jeff popped into my thoughts. I hadn't seen him in twenty years or so. It seemed odd that we hadn't found each other yet; the world had changed so rapidly since the nineties, but the force of social media had never rekindled our communication.

Jeff was up there with the people I was most grateful to. He had helped me immensely in that year of shock. I had tried to find him a few years prior, but to no avail.

My stubborn determination kicked in. I sat in front of the computer to find Jeff.

On my Internet deep-dive, I encountered a payment barrier and freely gave my credit card number. An address in North Liberty, Iowa came up.

I took my mom and my kids with me to Chicago for the midwinter convention, and on the way home, we detoured

DESTINED TO FAIL

to North Liberty. I knocked on the door of a house, and a boy answered.

"Is Jeff home?" I asked. The kid said no, but that that was his neighbor's name. He pointed to a house a few doors down. I knocked on Jeff's door, and another little boy answered.

"Is Jeff home?"

"One minute," said the boy. "Dad?"

Two seconds later, Pepperoni Pizza Jeff stood before me. He instantly did a double take. "Anas?"

I called everyone in the truck over to meet him. Then, we all sat together in Jeff's kitchen and talked for twenty minutes. Jeff had married his high school sweetheart, Beth, and now had a son and a daughter. I filled up on the joy of seeing a long-lost, important friend. Jeff and I hugged before my family piled into the truck again, and we drove home.

One day in the spring, I padded around the house, doing my rounds and folding laundry. *House Hunters* murmured on the television. The kids were zoned out on the couch.

When I passed the TV, I stopped. The face of the realtor looked oddly familiar. A ghost materialized. My jaw dropped.

"Is that guy named Carlos?" I asked my kids.

"Yeah," they said.

"Is that... Panama?"

"Yeah."

On the show, Carlos walked around in a suit. An American couple was at his heels, gazing wide-eyed at a house with east-facing windows. A wave of shock rushed over me.

I had never stopped looking for him. We'd tried to keep in touch in the nineties, but it had become too difficult. In college, we'd seen each other every day, whether through soccer or in the international students' office, or just driving around.

Carlos had been as broke as I was. During his second year, when he'd moved from his host family into the dorms, we'd split burgers in half, or I'd bring him leftovers from the restaurant. It saddened me to have lost touch. Now, my friend was on TV. *Unbelievable*.

I Googled Carlos and found his realtor profile online. His face shone up at me, light glinting off his cheeks. I sent him an email.

Carlos wrote an enthusiastic response. We Skyped each other, and the first conversation we had rolled on for five hours.

"You've gotta come to Panama," Carlos said.

"Hopefully, someday soon," I replied. I had wanted to see Carlos again since the day I saw him off to the gate.

In May 2014, Debbie said she had to talk to me. "Not at the lab," she told me. "Let's grab a sandwich."

DESTINED TO FAIL

We each bought lunch and a water at the Subway next door. I slid into a booth and sat across from Debbie as she covered the table with papers. She shuffled them in a focused trance, her sandwich lying untouched in front of her.

Numbers irritated me.

"You know I hate paperwork," I said, aggravated. "I don't want to look at my bills. Just give me the short of it."

Debbie looked up at me. She smiled.

"Go buy a car."

I nearly choked. Gingerly, I put down my sandwich.

"Excuse me?"

"We paid off all our debt," she said.

"*All* those credit cards?"

"Paid off."

"*All* the equipment loans?"

Debbie nodded.

"You mean it's all gone?" I asked.

"Yeah," Debbie reassured me. "It's all gone."

Time lost its relevance. The floor beneath my feet gave way; the booth evaporated. The dull murmur of the patrons, the radio, the hum of cars outside silenced in my ears. Something lifted in me.

The day after, I went to see an old friend, a local car dealer. We made small talk as I looked around at his selection of cars. It was quite high-end. A shiny white car caught my eye.

I excused myself and stepped to the side. I called Debbie.

"Hey, you knew what I meant by 'go buy a car,' right?" I asked.

"You have no more debt," Debbie said.

"Right."

"Right."

"So… I'm gonna buy a car," I said.

"Buy whatever you want. You're good to go."

I walked up to the dealer and pointed at the car I liked. "How much do you want for it?"

In the first mornings afterward, I still awoke with knots of worry. When I remembered that everything was all right, I settled into an unusual serenity.

Reality, after years of grief and stress and rage, released its toxins. The good news felt surreal.

DESTINED TO FAIL

THE PIRATE

By June 2014, my family had tried several times to mend the fractured relationship between me and my dad. I was stubborn and embittered. A custody battle still consumed me, but I was debt-free, and every day felt like I rose an inch from the ground. Still, I knew how much strength the confrontation would take. My limbs felt weak; my jaw ached. My mind and heart were tired, too. To stand before my father felt monumental. I needed time to amass the courage.

My older brother called one day.

"You can't continue to not talk to Dad. We're going to fix this," he said.

In Middle Eastern culture, families are tiered systems. The patriarch is right by default, and the youngest child is always wrong. My older brother felt it was his duty to mend the relationship. He was the religious one, the peacemaker. After five years in Dubai, where he had been assigned for work, he returned to Missouri. He told me he was going to drive over and mediate.

When I saw Natasha, she parsed the issue with me without knowing everything. Her mere presence helped. The phone call and the conversations made me introspective.

My gaze turned inward. I considered where I cast blame and why. *Why am I so angry all the time? So miserable?* I analyzed the extent of it and tried to find where it stemmed from.

My father's words were one thing. But they were nothing compared to how I spoke to myself. Failure seemed to arise in every area of my life. If I made less money than the day before, my outlook darkened. When my soccer team lost, even when we were on a winning streak, I blamed myself. I always had to be better. My inner critic was always the victor. As a human being, I did just fine. I was an expert dental technician, a good father, a fearsome athlete, a loyal friend. But a positive light couldn't permeate my cruel self-image. I haunted my own life. I never let myself breathe.

My brother and I met at our parents' house in Omaha. He wanted to bear witness and make certain my dad and I didn't continue our silence. My older brother and my parents sat on one end of the table. I sat alone, opposite them.

"Both of you, say your piece," said my brother.

I vented. Something had resolved with the absolution of my debt. Strength broadened my shoulders. The relief let courage in. I could face my father without feeling like a failure in his eyes. My family knew about the divorce, but I'd never told anyone the extent of it. I omitted the details but made certain they heard me.

My father laid out his own feelings. All I wanted was an acknowledgement of the abandonment, of the suffering he caused. I never received it. My father didn't think he had abandoned me in the first place, so of course he never thought what he'd done to me was wrong. He was fixated on the ends and never thought of the means.

But expressing myself was a release. My father and I shook hands and hugged.

In light of being debt-free, I booked four tickets to fly to Panama City. Carlos had invited me and my family. I tucked an Ace of Base CD into my carry-on bag.

Work tended to settle by the end of June. Natasha, the kids, and I flew to Central America at the end of the month in 2014.

When we arrived, Carlos pulled up to where we stood at the terminal. Twenty years had nothing on our friendship. We shouted and gripped each other's shoulders and embraced. I introduced Carlos to my family, then he helped us with our bags and pulled out of the terminal. On the road, he and I couldn't stop smiling and peering over at each other. Neither of us believed this was real.

I fiddled with the stereo. "What are you doing?" Carlos asked.

The Sign album began to play, and we were transported to 1993. Carlos grinned. Two grown men pumped their fists in the air to Ace of Base and belted out the words. Natasha and the kids looked at us funny.

Carlos and the kids

DESTINED TO FAIL

Panama City was lush and modern. Below the high-rises were sandy colonial exteriors. Elegant fingers of palm trees drummed the stagnant summer air.

Carlos took us to see the Panama Canal, like we'd talked about in college. I could sit on beaches with fine, white sand between my toes and not worry. My kids had fun, and it made me glad.

On our last day in Panama, the feeling of parting from a friend proved its lasting presence. I threw my arms around Carlos and thought about how much I detested goodbyes.

To be a single dad was to be a juggler. I drove my kids to and from school, fed them, worked a hundred-hour week, and somehow made time to spend with them. I paid for winter coats and sneakers, packed lunches for field trips, and looked over their shoulders at their math homework. It was taxing.

There were gaps in my instinct that only a mother would understand. Enforcing the rules from afar was the most difficult. One kid might step out of line, and I would scold them for it.

"But I'm at so-and-so's house," they would plead.

"The rules don't just apply when you're with me," I said. "They are in effect everywhere."

If one of them did something disagreeable, I criticized them. My kids listened to me. I knew they were going through something difficult, and as much as they needed someone to tell them what to do, the kids needed my love. I broke the curse of all the fathers before me, and I softened. I was openhearted and caring, and my children were better for it.

When I dropped them off at their grandparents' house, I worried they would talk about me or about how unstable they felt. But somehow, my kids remained quiet on the matter.

Once my dad and I had repaired our relationship, I took Natasha to meet my parents. She had been to the house a few times and knew my mom, but somehow had never met my dad. They both liked her and welcomed her instantly. I never gave air to my issues: the financial struggles, the custody, the divorce. Still, they saw I worked hard and needed support.

"I just want you to know," I said to my dad, "I'm happy in life. But you can help me with the kids."

My dad nodded, his brow furrowed. "Bring them over to the house. Anytime you want."

My thoughts were economic. I was responsible for the expenses of two homes: theirs and the condo. I paid two mortgages and two electricity bills. I mowed two lawns.

"Why don't I buy one big house?" I said. "You're both getting older. And I need a hand."

My dad nodded. "I like this idea," he said, solemnly. "I accept."

DESTINED TO FAIL

Suhair called me and asked if I was crazy. But I prided myself on my ability to compartmentalize.

I sold the condo and made some money from the renovated basement. One loan after another had been paid off; it felt good to release the violent grip the debt had had on my psyche.

I turned to Stan for another loan, to buy the big house.

"You're pre-approved," he said.

Contentment came in all colors.

My parents moved in with my kids and me in July 2014. My parents' presence, along with the knowledge that my kids were protected, was the mental boost I needed. I didn't worry if my children were alone. I trusted those four eyes watching over them.

The divorce still impacted Nader and Danah. I was not oblivious. Two important people and a house had been swiftly tugged out from under their feet when they were quite small. "Home" was always too strong a word.

I'd tried everything in my power to hold their world together. The condo had been a step toward the ideal. The house with my parents was a big leap. In their goings back and forth between their mom and me, they often referred to the two houses. Their mom's house tended to be closer to their idea of home. When they moved in with my family, out of habit, they still referred to it as a house. I shook my head.

"This is your *home*," I emphasized.

Nader and Danah each had the sanctity of a room to themselves. They warmed up to the idea of feeling stable in a permanent dwelling. This was *home*.

My children saw who I was in the context of the other fathers they knew. When the other dads were kicking up their feet to watch the football game, their dad had the light on at 3:00 in the morning, focused on his task until his eyes gave in. Other dads put their mattress to use. Nader and Danah barely saw me sleep.

The custody battle dragged on. Shanna and I hired handsomely paid professional bullies. The lawyers charged each other, and their clients by extension, for bitter letters that spewed words of hatred, hooded in dense, legal rhetoric. The brunt of the financial weight was on my shoulders. I supported my kids. I paid for my big, bad lawyer. In addition, I scrounged for the money to pay child support. Amidst these distractions, Shanna announced an engagement.

When I picked up my kids from school one day, they told me the news. I meditated on the event. I knew what would happen: she and her fiancé would buy a house together. She would sell the house I had put a down payment on and pocket the money.

Fighting was tiring. I gave all my money to the culprit in my misfortune, and I occupied a purgatory she commanded. Her hand had a central role in its creation.

But I deserve peace. Even she *deserves peace.*

I called her. "I need to talk to you. Could we meet somewhere?"

I could hear her flinch on the other end of the phone.

"It's okay," I said. "We'll be civil. Really."

Shanna agreed.

We met in a fast-food chain and sat across from each other. Shanna looked at me. Tense. Expecting an outburst.

"Here's the deal," I said. "You're getting married. You're buying a house, which you're going to use my money toward. Since we split, I've been paying for everything. I pay child support, and I support the kids."

Shanna blinked.

"So, be an adult," I said. "End all of this. Think of how much you're spending on lawyers, how much we both are. I'm tired, and I'm sure you are, too. I want to be done. We need to live separate lives."

Shanna nodded.

"I want full custody," I said. I didn't spare her the candor. "It's been my plan all along to make you waste your money. I'll never stop. I'll hire two lawyers, if I have to. I don't want anything from you, either. Not that thirty grand, not child support. Just full custody."

She let out a sigh. "Okay."

I ran to the coffee machine the next morning and paid no heed to my scalded throat as I drove to the lawyer's office. When I burst in, the secretary was caught off guard.

"Can I help you?"

"Yeah," I said. "I need thirty seconds of my lawyer's time. Right now."

She was ruffled. "Do you have an appointment?"

"No. I just need to see him." The secretary gave me a look before she fetched the lawyer. The Great White Shark walked out of his office.

"Shanna's gonna sign the custody papers," I blurted out. "I'm getting full custody."

The lawyer was dumbstruck. "You're… You're going to need to get those forms notarized."

"It's not a problem," I said.

Shanna had a certified notary where she worked. At lunch hour, I brought her the forms, and she signed them. The notary's stamp sounded the mighty hammer of a closure long desired. I drove back to my lawyer, the forms neatly stowed in a folder.

The Great White Shark couldn't believe it. He carefully inspected the signed paperwork then looked up at me, concerned.

"As your lawyer," he said, solemnly, "I have to ask you. Did you hold this woman at gunpoint?"

I chuckled. The lawyer was stony.

"No," I said. "I didn't."

Soon after, the Shark's firm sent me an email that Shanna's lawyer had filed a motion to withdraw. She and I established a schedule where we had equal time with the kids. I was fair and wasn't going to keep them from her. The

DESTINED TO FAIL

Great White Shark had helped significantly. But ultimately, I had won my kids back. My strategy of persistence paid off.

I finally had control and held onto the satisfaction of it.

The women of the old Ace lab were conservative. When I'd wanted to take risks, they'd held me back and clicked their tongues. Rebecca and Shanna were frightened by their inexperience, and to an extent, I was as well. When everything fell down around me, Debbie's accounting experience and smarts came to the rescue. I didn't argue with her.

To trust anyone after what happened was scary, but she had been a reliable force for good when I needed it most. Although I was the only person at Ace who signed the checks, my faith and respect for her was deeper than anyone I'd worked with.

A small error in a case was not the end of the world. One dentist in particular liked to blow up over minute details. I had warned him his disrespectful squabbles were unwelcome. Sure enough, the doctor lost his patience again. I said, "I'm not going to tolerate this." I ditched rude clients and renovated everything: my relationships, my business, and the points of intersection. I built a new workplace on a system of respect.

The dental world is run by doctors. They flash their hefty degrees and pearly whites. They walk all over labs like mine. I had seen the doctors as kings and myself as the subject. But I was older now. Tougher. *The doctor might be the king. But I'm the pirate.* I was a free entity. I breathed. My mind rearranged itself. I began again, savvier than before, in a structure where I felt safe enough to wing it.

Carlton and his family had grown closer to mine over the years. He liked to say that he had a son in Omaha. Carlton's daughter Deborah called me one day.

"You might want to drive to Des Moines as soon as possible."

The Tiramisu Club, 2015

DESTINED TO FAIL

That same day, I drove with Natasha and the kids to the home where Carlton had been cared for in his old age. They wouldn't let anyone in except family, but we all were ushered into the room right away. I saw Betty and her husband sitting beside Carlton, who was still sharp and in animated conversation with everyone there.

My family and I sat and spoke with him for a while. In the late afternoon we drove back to Omaha. Two days later, Carlton passed away.

We all mourned him, and I deeply felt the loss. Carlton was one of several people who'd been selfless, who'd offered their hand to help me in a period of urgency. I never forgot his kindness, half a lifetime later. Nader and I were now the last members of the Tiramisu Club.

In August, I went back to Jordan with Natasha and the kids. This time, I was satisfied to be home. Razi and I reunited. For eight days, the four of us, along with Razi and his family, toured the country. We went to Petra and participated in the normal tourist rites. We watched the sun set over Wadi Rum, where formations sprang from a brilliant orange desert and vermilions became magentas as darkness descended. We stayed at a resort in Aqaba and blissfully floated in the Dead Sea again. The family, sunny and sweet, welcomed us.

I was in my element again and roamed the city with the same street-smart confidence. In the two instances of my return as an adult, I noticed the drastic changes Amman had undergone. There was a home here, one I loved and had been unfairly driven from. There was also my home across the ocean, one I had worked hard to establish and hold on to. In Jordan, I was an American. In America, I was a foreigner. Natasha and the kids saw the conflict in me. At that moment, I wasn't sure where home was.

A job and a life still demanded a great deal of me. Even the Americans were sad to leave. Natasha and the kids were teary, and I was, too. I hugged Razi, and we bid the family farewell. All of us would run away to Jordan if we could.

The family in downtown Amman

DESTINED TO FAIL

Riding a camel in Petra

THE LAUNCH

When I was seventeen, a sentiment fluttered between my mother and my cousin: "He's good with his hands." Like my Latin grandpa, I made jewelry, though it was only a hobby. My customers were Danah, Natasha, my mother, and close friends. Most of all, I liked to make rings: bling for the pinky of a gangster who cursed and smoked big cigars. Or a vine of silver whose ends barely met before curling the other way. I loved tangible, handmade things.

My search for engagement rings was overwhelming. Most were stupid expensive and, regardless of the price, ultimately impersonal. I browsed shops and boutiques with Natasha on a trip we took. "That ring is really pretty," she said, eyeing something unique. I stored a picture of it in my mind.

I tinkered away at a band of white gold. It was an interim ring, but my soul would be in it. I could have easily used something conventional, like a diamond, but decided on a rare gem that happened to be Natasha's birthstone. I

DESTINED TO FAIL

called my friend Dustin at the custom gem store. "What are the chances you could find me an alexandrite?"

He made a few calls and reached some guys in New York who had one. He told me the dimensions of the stone. I knew the measurements of the ring. Without seeing the rock, I said, "Buy it."

Dustin incorporated the alexandrite into the metal. I tucked the ring away in a box, snug within a pocket hidden in the depths of a bag, before Natasha and I boarded the plane to California. To see Cousin Ziad was the ruse. The mission itself was to propose and watch Ziad perform on New Year's Eve.

It all was slightly overwhelming. The speech I'd practiced. The handmade, smuggled ring with the rare stone. I felt again like the kid who'd smuggled cigarettes all that time ago.

Like Brad Pitt *in Ocean's Eleven*, Zi ate constantly. He couldn't help but fall victim to his ardent yearning for food. When the morning I meant to propose arrived, we stood around in the kitchen, waiting for coffee. I gave Zi a meaningful look. He spoke to me in Arabic.

"Are you nervous?" he asked.

"Not really," I said. "But when we leave, we've gotta go straight there."

"Totally, man."

"When we get there, you distract her while I set up the video camera," I said. "I'm going to give you another camera to take pictures."

Zi agreed. Yet we were not halfway out the door when he uttered the words, "I'm hungry."

"No. Let's just go," I said, trying to sound unbothered.

The three of us piled into Zi's car. I touched the box in my pocket for reassurance. For five blocks, the car was quiet. Then, I heard a gasp from the backseat.

"Jamba Juice!" Natasha exclaimed.

Zi echoed her enthusiasm. As he pulled into the parking lot, I thought, *No, we don't want juice!*

Natasha ordered her usual green juice. I got an orange juice. After a lengthy deliberation, Zi ordered oatmeal, the only thing at the juice bar that required cooking. It took the kitchen ten minutes. I glared at my cousin, trying to contain my begrudging amusement as he savored each steaming bite.

When Zi finished his oatmeal, we got back on the road. It was thirty minutes to Palos Verdes. "No more ideas," I muttered to Zi.

The car was new; it smelled and cruised that way toward the bluffs atop the sea. We arrived and parked. The three of us walked to the edge of the cliff. While Natasha and I looked out at the view and inhaled the salty air, Zi stealthily walked a little ways behind us.

DESTINED TO FAIL

After a few seconds, I turned around. Zi had set up the video camera. He gave me a thumbs up, and I gave one in return. I began to recite my speech. My heart rose to my throat as I felt around for the box in my pocket. My knee planted itself on the earth. The ground on which she stood radiated with every little glory of her: Natasha, the best person I knew, whom I always wanted to know. I presented the ring and met her gaze, assured.

Natasha's eyes grew big, taking it in. She covered her mouth with her scarf.

Slowly, she lowered it. Natasha smiled wide. Pieces of grass from her green smoothie dotted her teeth.

"Yes!" she wholeheartedly exclaimed.

"You have green teeth," I said, laughing.

My proposal to Natasha

Zi's girlfriend joined us, and we went out to celebrate. Natasha couldn't believe it. Somehow, I couldn't, either. At the airport, we engaged in the ritual we'd performed for years. Our goodbye was a beginning. I went back to Omaha, and she to Denver.

The person I was during my first marriage was unsustainable: stressed, short-tempered, angry. I vowed to change. Warmth now permeated where empty lack of feeling had been before. My insides had grown void and lifeless and stayed that way for a long time. Now, my laughter felt full, and emotion filled my whole being. I wouldn't lose Natasha. I was strong enough to hold down a second marriage.

A member of the small dental community in Omaha told me that a lab called Larsen was struggling financially and looking to sell. They had rejected my application in 1997. "Insufficient experience," they'd said. I saw an opportunity to double the income at Ace and called up the owner of Larsen. I made an offer, and he accepted.

I called Stan, who knew I was good for it. He gave me a loan for half the purchase price, on the condition I would match every dollar. Stan trusted me. Though buying Larsen was a risk, I was unafraid now.

I whipped things into shape. Two employees from Larsen moved into Ace. The owner wanted to come on board, too, but I refused. Larsen was tangled up in itself and inefficiently operated. Authorities would inevitably collide.

Under my leadership, the workload doubled overnight. The majority of the accounts from Larsen liked the quality of the work and stayed. As the accounts doubled, so did the income. The gamble paid off. Ace began to make real money.

With Debbie's help, I was strategic about my finances. At the beginning of the year 2016, Debbie and I aimed to put some money away each month. I sandwiched what Stan gave me with a little income. The rest of what Ace brought in, I saved.

"If we have enough saved by September and pay everything off, we take the employees to Mexico," I emphatically proclaimed.

Debbie was enthusiastic, and she took me up on it.

Natasha and I didn't want a traditional wedding. The custom of holding weddings and funerals in the same space conflated birth and death. These were opposite ceremonies, and each required a separate, hallowed ground. If I were to get married again, I decided, it would be in the fresh air. And not in winter, the gray, blue season of dying things. It would be in spring or summer, with life humming in the trees.

While we dated, Natasha mused, "Someday, if I ever get married, I'd like it to be by the water." She arranged everything. Natasha had loved Punta Cana when we visited, and she made the ceremony there.

If we'd had it our way, Natasha and I would have gotten married just the two of us. But my kids had to be there, along with our parents. She invited about twenty people: everyone we loved, from my family to hers. Stacey, the reason we met, was there with bells on. Shelley came with her fiancé. Tony flew in.

Natasha found a pier that stretched a hundred feet from the beach. My friend, Lorenzo, officiated. My kids were there. My mom brimmed with pride. A breeze lifted shirtsleeves and teased the water. Caribbean guitars played. We said our vows over an emerald sea. I glowed with joy.

Me and Natasha, Just Married

DESTINED TO FAIL

A few people couldn't make it. Natasha and I didn't hold anything against them. It was a destination wedding after all, and not everyone could find it in their schedule or wallets. But nothing could bother us. Everyone had fun dancing and wandering around the town and getting a little sunburned on the bridge of their noses. The place glowed prominently in our memory. We would always return to Punta Cana.

I was working late one night in winter when Ziad called me. Natasha and I had seen Zi's proposal to his girlfriend on a balmy evening in Mexico.

"The wedding's in June! You and the family are invited."

"That's great!" I said.

"We have something to ask you," Zi said. "Would you officiate?"

"Who, me? Officiate?" I was speechless. "Yes, of course!" My brain did cartwheels. *What does that mean? Do I need a license?*

Over the next few months, I laid out a few sentences for a speech then shook my head in disapproval, my finger over the delete button. I fretted over what to say. I didn't want to ruin Zi's big night.

In February, after the annual midwinter convention in Chicago, I went to catch my 9 p.m. flight home and found it was postponed until 10:00 the next morning. The other passengers and I were put up on a row of uncomfortable cots in a wing of the airport. I couldn't sleep.

At 8 p.m., I fiddled on my phone. My eyes strained over the notes app as I typed out the speech. At 3:00 in the morning, I fell asleep.

Back in Omaha, I finished and edited the speech. Tony helped me; he was good with this kind of stuff. I registered as a wedding officiant. Zi, his fiancée, and Natasha were the only others who knew. I hinted at nothing.

The wedding overlooked the ocean. My mom, my kids, and my extended family sat near me in the front row. The ceremony began. A lull in the proceedings made the crowd look around and murmur about how there was no officiant.

Zi nodded in my direction. I whipped the speech from my jacket and stood up. A collective gasp from my family turned to laughter. The reception in the evening was full of dancing and good food, and Zi was happy.

Ziad's wedding, 2017

The year went by, and most things ran smoothly at Ace. When August came around, Debbie went through the books. Ace had made the cut to go to Mexico. Natasha looked up flights. The employee appreciation trip was all-inclusive: the flight there and back and the resort, too.

"Bring your boyfriend, your cat, your mom," I said. "But you have to pay for a plus one."

Natasha, the trip master, booked a flight to Mexico for everyone at the lab. We closed everything down and sent letters to our accounts, stating we would be out of office. Everyone from the lab came and brought someone along. I brought Natasha, my mom, and my kids with me. Debbie came, too.

On a Friday, the animated employees congregated at the terminal. Donning floppy sunhats, they chatted about work. Soon the subject changed to the trip.

As the whole of my company boarded the flight, an anxious thought crossed my mind. *If something happens to this plane, it's the end of the business.*

To my delight, the pilot didn't fall asleep at the controls. The company landed smoothly in Playa del Carmen. I stepped out into the mild, breezy warmth. Everyone let out a contented sigh.

For four days, my family and I sat by the water and basked in the sun. The flight back to Omaha was split two ways. Half the party made connections in Dallas, the other in Denver. My family made our connection in Denver, and Natasha and I parted ways. My kids and I boarded a plane back to Omaha. On the flight, they slept next to me, tired from the trip.

Pensive, I scrolled through the photo stream on my phone. A reel of sound and images played in my mind. Memories of the past six years, stuff that used to haunt me now gave me assurance. The adulterer in his suit, weathered and guilt-ridden. Debbie's face and the condemnation. "You're bankrupt." The totaled car, rammed into the ATM by a stranger who didn't know the depression I wrestled with. The rage I unleashed on my father. Tears of relief in the Fremont parking lot. Hunched over my workstation all the while. The exhaustion. Ceaseless.

The past dissolved into the white noise of the plane. The head of a sleeping child fell against my arm. The other slept against the cavernous wall by the window. *I just went to Mexico with my family and my entire crew.* I beamed.

Natasha and I continued as we always had. A long-distance relationship, though, required a tiring amount of planning and a maintenance of good communication, connection, and trust. Natasha and I felt it was worth it because of the demands of our individual lives, yet we missed out on the simple, daily joys of living together, and we missed each other. When I saw Natasha on weekends, she began to appear faint. She was tired. A depression had come over her.

She lived in a room in her father's house in Brighton, Colorado, which was a forty-five-minute commute to her job in Denver. I knew the toll a lack of a secure home had on a person. Life felt like an airport: liminal, anxious, teeming with uncertainty.

Natasha and I talked about buying a house in Denver. It would be ours and would give her a stable dwelling. She found some property in an up-and-coming neighborhood, where artists and hipsters had escaped the rising expenses of the city. The first time I went to Denver was in July 2000, to see Metallica at the Mile High Stadium. I'd loved it; the mountains and skyscrapers made Omaha look even smaller than it was. It was exactly the city in the States where I had imagined myself being. *I could totally live here,* I had thought.

I arrived to see the property. Stepping out of the car, I was wary. Natasha saw the look on my face, like I had forgotten my bullet-proof vest.

"Oh, it's *fine*," Natasha said. "Come look! This developer's gonna completely start over. If we get in now, it'll be so cheap. This will all be cleaned up, and the property will go up in value quickly. Trust me."

Natasha knew Denver, and I trusted her. We put a down payment on the place. Over the next year, the brittle skeleton of the foundation rose up from the ground. A finished product evolved in the slowly gentrifying neighborhood. I was impressed.

Something within Natasha settled. The dark circles vanished from under her eyes. Now, I could have a place to land when we saw each other in Denver. Natasha's house, the shared place, brought her peace. To be able to support her gratified me, too.

I looked to expand Ace Dental once again. The debt was long paid off. At the time, Ace only operated as a fixed lab:

we produced crowns and permanent dental fixtures. I wanted to become a full-service lab. This meant adding a removable department. (Grandpa's teeth, for example, are removable.)

I spoke with my landlord, who allowed us to start construction in a vacant section of the building. Without a word to anyone, I asked a dental technician who specialized in removables if she would come work for me. She agreed.

The new employee was my ex-wife.

I told Natasha and half-expected her to fly off the handle. But Natasha was always rational. This time was no different.

"Why?" she said. She had advocated for me to make peace with Shanna. Still, she questioned the decision.

I had a practical response.

Shanna worked a minimum-wage corporate job at an agricultural enterprise. I supported the kids, and she didn't offer much. Nader was preparing for college, and I was about to put a sizable deposit down. Shanna needed to make money, to give her support where it was due. I talked to her and her husband about the arrangement, and he was fine with it.

I compartmentalized. One side of my brain clung to my distrust toward her. The infidelity and embezzlement had plunged me into darkness. But I stored that information elsewhere. Work was my religion. I only cared about diligence and skill in my employees. Their character was secondary. I didn't like to admit it, but Shanna was good at her job. She wouldn't hold the same position of financial power. She wouldn't have the access. For now, if she made money, life would be easier.

Everyone had been informed of Shanna's character. My kids, conflicted, knew what had happened. I sat my family down and told them.

My parents and my kids stared at me, their faces blank. Their mouths hung open. I knew my parents' horror; adultery was the worst thing to them. My mom objected to the arrangement.

"She shouldn't be near you! You can't trust her."

My dad was the pragmatic one. He looked me in the eye. "Is this going to benefit you long-term?"

"Yes," I replied.

He nodded. "Do what you have to do."

My instinct was keen. The removable department was a lucrative addition to the business. Shanna's presence and her support relaxed the kids. They were happier. She and I split the kids' bills. College tuition wasn't as burdensome.

When Labor Day weekend came around, so did the annual appreciation trip to Mexico. My parents came along (my dad had a blast). Shanna and her husband came, too. It was a lesson for my kids. Shanna had matured since the divorce. She was their mother, and I knew she wanted to be close to them. She was as in love with these wonderful children as I was. I would make peace with her, for them and for my own inner stability.

In time, I understood the persuasive nature of the banker. He was the serpent who had willed Shanna to cheat and steal. He'd whispered diabolical falsehoods in her ear about me and empty promises of a future where they would all be together. When I'd met Shanna twenty-six years ago, I had been fresh from a year of reckless partying, running on hormones and soccer victories. I'd been over it, but Shanna had not been that way as a young person. The affair had been a beacon of the wild she felt had passed her by.

The more I reflected, the more I realized how the damage Shanna caused was a catalyst. It had forced me to reorder my approach to business, to finances, to my way of thinking. Shanna had torn up my life until it was rendered nearly unrecognizable. Still, I gazed in wonder at the good that grew from it. If it weren't for her destructive act, I would never have found Natasha, love of my life.

I was immensely proud of the people my children became. Responsible. Kind-hearted. Incredibly smart. I poured my everything into them.

When Nader turned seventeen, I was still in contact with a friend of mine from several years ago. While the divorce raged, I hit the bars with the guys on weekends. I needed the social interactions; they relieved and energized me. I had met my friend Ana on one of my excursions to the bar. She mentioned that she was from Spain.

"My mom's from Spain!" I said, excited, and we bonded. We had kept in touch since 2010. Ana and I devised an exchange plan: she would send her nephew, Alejandro, to the States for three weeks, and a little earlier, I would send Nader to Burgos in the north of the country, where Ana lived.

"When are we leaving?" Nader asked when he heard the news.

"No," I said. "The question is, when are *you* leaving?"

Nader was daunted by the idea of going alone, but excitement superseded his intimidation.

"I can do it," he said.

Natasha and I drove him to the airport in Denver. We watched him disappear through security. I didn't hold my son's hand, as my mom had done, twenty-five years before, on the other side of the world. I attempted to suppress my parental nerves.

Does he have everything? Will he make his gate? Will he make all his connections?

By this time, Nader was well-traveled, but he'd have to navigate Heathrow in London, an expansive and overwhelming airport, and find his connection to Madrid. Once he arrived in Madrid, Ana would be there to pick him up. *Is he gonna find her okay?*

What felt like three days passed before Ana texted me that he'd made it. *"Don't worry,"* she said. *"I've got him."*

He was safe. I exhaled. Nader had done all that by himself.

At the end of the two weeks, Ana and her family drove Nader south to Madrid, where he reunited with all of us. Ana and I saw each other for the first time since she'd left Omaha, and our two families met. Afterward, she saw all of us to our terminal. We flew to Tenerife and visited my relatives. On our return to the States, a jetlagged Nader looked at me.

"Dad," he said, "I've gotta say, going somewhere and walking around not knowing the language is really hard."

"Yeah," said the sage. "I may know a thing or two about that."

My kids with my mom in Spain, 2018

When I came home from work one day, my dad was sitting in the kitchen. He called a hello as I walked in.

"How was your day?" he asked.

I replied. We talked of nothing for a while, until I asked about my relatives on my ongoing quest for ancestral knowledge.

My dad didn't speak of his parents. He told me the story of my maternal grandparents, of my grandmother, Isabel. He recalled how they came to Tenerife and how my grandfather met my grandmother. For a while, my dad spun yarns on the Latin family. He recalled himself as a young man on his honeymoon, and how the Spanish family had welcomed him.

My parents on their honeymoon

When my mom walked in, she told stories, too. For forty-five minutes, the three of us talked around the kitchen table.

I enjoyed these conversations. They were new and serendipitous. Originally, it had been for pragmatic reasons that my parents moved in; to be financially prudent and offer a hand with my children. But my dad and I had spent stretches of our lives apart.

The vision we had of living under the same roof again was more profound than I'd comprehended. We gradually caught up with each other for missed time and unaccounted truths.

ANAS AFANA & STELLA BELLOW

GOOD INTENTIONS

I remembered, in the misty recesses of my brain, when dusk threatened itself over a bankless river. How my friends and I packed up our picnic on the island in the middle of the Nile. We'd never feared the dark water, which crawled with monstrous reptiles. As it always was, the benevolent fisherman had spotted us before we saw his boat come over the horizon. He gave us a ride back to the mainland. We paid him a little, overflowing with gratitude.

I reappeared to my mom, grubby and smiling, and pacified her with white lies. I lay in bed that night and envisioned our next trip. The next morning, Ali would pick me up. I would daydream my classes away. My friends, who were many, would wait for me. Work was a foreign concept.

This child's life was easy, one most children only envied from afar. I could go anywhere, do anything. I could have wild adventures on the Nile and be reassured of a soft place to land. A father to provide for me, a mother to love me and cook and feed me good things. I dreamt, unencumbered.

DESTINED TO FAIL

Running through fields, wind whistling by my ears and tousling my hair. I was an athlete, a seeker of absolute freedom.

My adult self felt cut off from this person. I was so far removed from my adolescent self, I deemed it a past life. My evolution had been arduous. An abrupt entry into the United States was a hindrance to my development. Dreams and stability had been thrown into chaos. I'd had to work to regain what I had of myself.

I thought about the days, two and a half years apart, when my son and daughter were born. They became my singular focus. My drives to work and provide all stemmed from their existence and dependence on me. I didn't want to fail as a father. I opened myself up and got close to them, something my father was never able to do.

Some people refused to express love and invented ways to bury it. In my father's generation, they called it "tough love." I couldn't handle it. I took things to heart. As a kid, I envied my friends for their thick skin. They deflected derision like it was nothing. I made friends with everyone, but the closest ones were the straight-shooters. To me, words were magnets. They meant everything; they informed the way I saw myself. My father's words were a plague on my existence.

On that August day in the college parking lot, I had been condemned by my father: "You were destined to fail." In that moment, I'd summoned a resistance. My entire being—heart, bones, cells, atoms—would not let me fail.

I'd scrubbed dishes, forged documents, wrecked cars, and spent drawn-out hours over my bench. The reconstruction of my personal life, the dauntless rescue of the business from bankruptcy had all been to prove I could outrun failure. I could never let my father think he was right. "Destined to fail" was the refrain of a melody, a song I knew by heart. It took two decades to rid myself of it.

My father's early retirement from the ambassador position was all political. The man they chose over him was in bed with the higher-ups. My dad had made money, but he'd worked for the Jordanian government. The position was one thing. For an ambassador, the salary was modest.

He had supported my three older siblings: my eldest sister's tuition for medical school, my brother's engineering education in the United States, and my sister's sociology degree. For the eight or nine years before he was out of a job, although my dad was financially drained, he wasn't worried about me. But, out of nowhere, the government forced him to retire at age fifty-five. The beginnings of the Gulf War had threatened the tiny country where he lived. He'd needed to get his kid out of the Middle East. And I needed an education far from Jordan.

My brother had come to the States in 1984. My uncle, the professor, had watched over him with a benevolent eye as he studied. But my dad could no longer travel the world with his family. He never imagined they'd retire him so soon. The money wasn't there for him to offer more support. My father wanted the best for me, but there was only so much to give.

I only knew how great my father's love was through my mom. While she liberally doled out her own affections, she often repeated how much my dad loved me. He expressed his care through hard work, stability, and financial support. Perhaps my older siblings had a different experience, but I couldn't access this love. Even though he once held a position of influence, he couldn't support me as I struggled in a foreign country. Dad's love would remain elusive. I'd had to go it on my own.

Three years into living in the new house with my parents, I came home late one night. As I prowled the fridge for a snack to heat up before bed, my dad padded into the kitchen. He sat across the table as I ate and asked about work.

We talked as 11:00 bled into midnight. One subject led to another. Before either of us knew it, my father told me the story of his childhood, which I had never heard.

"I was born and raised in the village of Malha," my dad began. "When I was eight, in 1948, our village fled in the Nakba. My parents took all they could," he said. His face fell, and he looked somewhere distant. "We lost everything."

"I remember the cave we lived in for months on end," he continued. "We hoped beyond anything that we could return home. But it became clearer that it wasn't safe for us anymore. We found a temporary home in the village of Hindaza and eventually settled in Bethlehem, where I finished high school. I graduated top of my class and was the only one to receive a full-ride scholarship to the American University in Beirut."

My dad told me he received a BA in Political Science. Afterward, he moved to Jordan, where he applied and was accepted into the Ministry of Foreign Affairs. The Ministry sponsored his studies for a year at Columbia University, where he took some courses on international law. After his time in New York, my dad went back to Jordan and climbed his way through the ranks of the embassy.

Pretty impressive for a guy who spent a year living in a cave, I thought.

As I brushed my teeth before bed, I pondered what a childhood in exile could do to a person. I'd had to be tough, like my dad had had to be tough before me. Already, though, I had withdrawn the blame and resentment I'd held and transmuted it into a form of reconciliation with my own wounds.

The figure of my father, once so vivid and terrifying in my mind, had vanished. I recognized my mental conflict. My dad had become separate from it.

Me and my dad

Once, I said to my dad, "You were forced to go to Jordan. You also forced me to come here, to the United States."

"Correct." He nodded and said nothing more.

Ultimately, my dad was right. Who would I be, had I not been left to fend for myself in the cornfields? In an odd way, being forced to come to the States was the best thing to happen. My naïveté had blocked out my father's true motive. I was sent to a better place, for a better life.

I loved Jordan; it would always be home or part of that elusive idea. After my thirty years in the States, although I worked until my back gave out, I had gratitude for this country. It gave my family a good life. At seventeen, when my soccer dreams were crushed, my disappointment had felt all-consuming. It was hard to see the good intention in my father.

PASS THE BATON

The house where we lived was big and sunny. My dad rose with the birds. He made his coffee and watched the sun paint the neighbor's roof golden. He held a peach under the cold, running water. He gently peeled the sticker from the skin and placed it by my car keys. Then he padded off, back to his room.

Sometimes, I saw him in the mornings before work. We held polite conversations in the kitchen while I drank my coffee. Other times, I found a piece of fruit in a small puddle on the counter next to my keys. I figured Dad had gone back to bed.

I recalled a blue feeling at the base of my stomach. It recurred throughout my life. The feeling was towering, unconquerable. I felt it when Mustafa disappeared into the unknown, when Jeff and Carlos left, when Shanna was unfaithful, and when Rebecca quit. When the business fell into ruin. It was most acute when I was alone, staring at the ceiling.

At age seventeen, I'd had little perspective. Life was an inordinate expanse of heartbreak, euphoria, and chagrin. The arc was almost impossible to make sense of. But now I saw a transitory nature in all things. The joy, the friends, the discomfort, the failure—they were all relative. They were small dots, blinking in and out of focus in the wide sea of all things.

I recalled the different places I'd seen from airplane windows. A veiny metropolis, a barren desert, a plain swallowed by deluge. I felt a weight in my stomach when I knew nothing about a foreign land.

My abandonment in the Midwest had jolted my system. Being seventeen only slightly eased that. I was young then and therefore better equipped to pick up the language and make new friends. Still, the world felt jarring. Culture shock exacerbated the hardship. The holidays in the States were different. The customs and the weather were cold and inhospitable. The adjustment took years.

My sources of comfort were people: close friends, who were kind and reliable and made the alien climates forgiving. Communication enabled me to attract good souls. Jeff, Tony, Carlton, Natasha—they anchored me; they eased the shock, the hardship, and the hurt. Benevolence rushed to my aid when I needed it most.

I poured goodness into my relationships. Ace Dental thrived. Love, in this union, was deeper and more true. Natasha and I livened it with humor, loyalty, and mutual support. I made peace with my ex-wife for the sake of our kids. My friends, my children, and my soulmate were compassionate, and they allowed me to summon that within myself.

At seventeen, I was forced to reckon with a new life. A multitude of obstacles lay in wait. Some were situational; others, bureaucratic. I worked hard, and often it felt fruitless. I wrestled with fear and loneliness. For a long time, life was hellish. Meaning was lost on me.

Some touted the American Dream. Others declared it unobtainable. I sat somewhere in the middle. During my first years in the United States, I knew nothing about it. In retrospect, the concept only hit me when I had achieved it for myself. I took issue with the term, a romanticism of the idea that, before, had clouded my vision. The obstacles were a maze I had to navigate in order to obtain anything worthwhile. I remembered how treacherous that journey was. *To accomplish the American Dream,* I thought, *you must first survive the Nightmare.*

I attained survival, fighting for a sense of stability, first for myself, and again for my children. At an easier time, I could look beyond myself.

My two kids, one born in summer and one in winter, transformed into polar opposite adults. One was sanguine and spirited, while the other was thoughtful and grounded. Each of them was wise and driven in their own respects. My own work ethic was their influence.

My mom had always said I would be the family dentist, but the role skipped a generation. Nader currently studies chemistry at the University of Nebraska Lincoln and is part of the Air Force ROTC program there. He is on the path to becoming a dentist.

Danah studies marketing at the University of Nebraska Omaha. She has always had a head for business and has a tremendous work ethic: over the summers, she sometimes works up to three jobs. Danah never settles, constantly looking for the next thing to satiate her unquenchable ambition.

Unlike my father, I was always present and empathetic to my kids. I still insisted on my high expectations. Nader and Danah were first-generation—they had a responsibility to work hard and maintain the stability I'd secured. This was important to me, as someone who went through tremendous hardship to find a comfortable life.

When you are unceremoniously thrust into a foreign land, you learn the value of selflessness. Selfless people saved my life.

What mattered—before success or money or stability—was the character of my kids. I wanted Nader and Danah to be self-sufficient and successful because I loved them. In a fatherly sense, I demanded they learn compassion and selflessness. When either of them expressed these qualities, I was proud.

DESTINED TO FAIL

The American Dream is a great accomplishment. It is a race, a passing of a flaming torch that every wretched soul who enters this country must carry tirelessly, some until they die.

My remarkable children are the next ones in the relay. I know they are strong enough to see it through.

ANAS AFANA & STELLA BELLOW

ACKNOWLEDGMENTS

The creation of this book was hugely collaborative. An enormous thank you to the following:

Natasha Afana, for her thorough feedback and ongoing, loving support of this project. Scott Reiling, not only for his thoughtful and consistent edits of the manuscript, but for encouraging Anas to write his memoir—it was more than worth it.

Anas's children, Nader and Danah, for their testimonies, feedback, and moral support. Mohammed Afana, for his interview on his experiences as a diplomat and the geopolitical climate, and for every one of his stories, especially the one about his childhood and his testimony of the Nakba.

Siham Afana, for giving us excellent information and details about events. Amelia Reiling, for getting the project off the ground and editing throughout the process. Samantha Joy, our guide throughout the journey of finalizing and publishing the book, for her wisdom, encouragement, and support. Kathryn Galán, for her crucial developmental edits, copy editing, and formatting the book for publication.

Issam Affaneh, for his beautiful insights. Heather Bellow, for toning down the flowery stuff and helping with the better beginning. Wayne Rasmussen, for copyrighting the content and giving us great feedback.

Anas's good friends, for their beautiful testimonies of him: Tony Buccheri and Maurizio Gagliolo. Brandi Nowak Dalton, for her support and investment in this book. The talented dentist and artist Trent Tobler, for the gorgeous portrait. Pixel Studios for cover design.

James Hetfield, Ace of Base, and Beyonce Knowles Carter, for getting us through the difficult and the surreal.

And thank you to the Universe, for doing its thing.

To dive deeper into Anas's story and to stay updated on Anas's and Stella's travels and events, please visit:

DestinedToFailBook.com

ANAS AFANA & STELLA BELLOW

ABOUT THE AUTHORS

Anas Afana owns a dental lab in Omaha, Nebraska, and has two grown children, Nader and Danah, who are now in college. He travels between the Heartland and Denver, where he spends time with his wife, Natasha. This is his first book.

Stella Bellow is an artist and writer with a BFA in Illustration and Literature at The New School in New York City. Originally, she hails from the ancient hills and woodlands of the Berkshires, where she spends her summers working and creating. This is her first book.

Made in the USA
Las Vegas, NV
04 January 2023